Character Building Acronyms

The ABC'S at Work*

*We Only Respect Kindness

By

Bruce Brummond

Character Building Acronyms: The ABC'S at Work, Bruce Brummond

Brummond, Bruce

Library of Congress Control Number: 2007928784

ISBN-10: 0-9788486-2-4
ISBN-13: 978-0-9788486-2-0

Printed in the United States of America

Welcome

This activities book is intended to be used after reading *Acronyms Building Character: The ABCs of Life,* by Bruce Brummond. The exercises are crafted for helping adults and young adults individually or in group settings to lead more successful lives. Hundreds of words, indelibly defined by their unique acronyms, are strategically listed to further enable you to comprehend, retain, and apply the methodology.

By completing this activities book you will be better equipped to:

Appreciate yourself

Renew your passion for life

Turn your stress into strengths

Learn to include fun in all that you do

Discover the ingredients of personal happiness

Enhance your vision of self worth by redirecting habits

Comprehend your desire to belong, to be needed, and to be loved

Understand how to balance your purpose, pleasure, and peace of mind

Acquire lasting insights into productive interpersonal relationships

Empower those around you to communicate and cooperate

Establish actions for unity, morale, loyalty, and pride

Help understand success and satisfaction

Develop positive, "can-do" attitudes

Learn how to achieve goals

Nourish your soul

LEADERSHIP MODULE—"I CARE about Teamwork"

To experience the "Leadership Module" simply complete the chapters in the order that spells out *"I CARE"—Integrity, Communication, Attitude, Respect, and Empowerment—*plus *Teamwork.*
Then enjoy the remaining chapters in the order that best suits your needs.

The entire workbook can be used in the workplace, all types of organizations, in addition to University, High School, and Middle School curriculums. You might consider acronyms, individual exercises, or specific chapters for personal exercises, small group sessions, family activities, or at organizational training sessions. Incorporating portions of this material in group meetings can certainly enhance the regular agenda.

Success is much more than a place, it is a JOURNEY*

***J**oyous **O**pportunities **U**nleashing **R**enewal **N**ow **E**mpower **Y**ou

Dedicated to the memory

of

Robert A. Moawad

Bob's passion for helping others realize their potential has painted an indelible imprint upon the planet. His modeling of creativity, hard work, family, friendships, and faith has elevated all who have been blessed by his presence.

Mr. Moawad perpetually exemplified his leadership among leaders by personally enacting the principles that he so fervently espoused. The wisdom and goodness that he so tirelessly shared will forever remain in the hearts of millions.

Contents

Preface

You are looking at an absolute gem of a tool for improving interactions with your family, friends, and career associates. This newly developed methodology is simply an amazing "crash course" in becoming a better human being.

Bruce has constructed lessons in *Character Building Acronyms* that reflect and expand upon the essence of the messages that are so masterfully introduced in his book *Acronyms Building Character*. These exercises will allow you to internalize the concepts which will help transform the dynamics of your relationships to make living and loving more fulfilling than ever imagined.

We at Snap-On Tools have used training programs developed by the "best of the best" in the human resources development industry. We are now including *Acronyms Building Character* and *Character Building Acronyms* in our toolbox to help us strengthen our leadership capacity, become even better managers, employees, family members, friends and overall better people.

I highly recommend that you make use of Brummond's methods for enhancing personal and organizational integrity. His common sense approach, intertwined with witty acronyms, is entertaining, easy to understand, and apply. You will learn to better get along with yourself and your world while developing your skills to experience a more fulfilling and successful life.

Jeff Howe
National Sales Manager
Snap-On Tools, Inc.

The Character Building Acronyms workbook answer key is located at...

www.characterconstructioncompany.com

CHANGE
Certain Habits Always Negatively Ground Everyone

- ## CONNECT
  Let's have a check up from the neck up!

  The first requirement for change is setting a _____ (Goodness Only Awaits Labor)

  and having a _____ (Does Everyone Strive In Reaching Excellence) to attain that

  change. _____ (Sure Tough Regularly Exercising Self-Sacrifice) is created when

  things change around us and we _____ (Notice Everyone's Esteem Develop) to

  _____ (Always Developing Attitudes Providing Trust) to a new _____

  (Very Intense Statement Indicating Objectives Necessary). Feel _____ (Feel Renewed

  Empowerment Everyday) to _____ (Always Seek Knowledge) others for

  _____ (Hurry Everybody Loves Progress) so you _____ (Character

  Advances Nobility) have the _____ (Seek Understanding Carefully Character

  Eventually Sows Satisfaction) that you _____ (Wishes Always Need Time) and you can

  be _____ (Have All the Peace'n Pleasure Y'want).

- ## CHALLENGE
  Deciding what needs to change in your life

  1. Let's look at what is required to balance your purpose, pleasure and peace of mind. These elements certainly may be entwined in more than one category.

  ➢ List three things in priority order that give you a feeling of purpose.

  _____

  _____

  _____

➤ List three things in priority order that give you pleasure.

_____

_____

_____

➤ List three things in priority order that give you peace of mind.

_____

_____

_____

• CHANNEL
Deciding which elements are the most important

1. Establishing the importance of the elements in your life:

➤ From the previous listings prioritize four important ingredients in your life:

_____

_____

_____

_____

(Are the things you listed to balance your purpose, pleasure, and peace of mind in the order that you would like them to be in? It might be beneficial to revisit this exercise after you complete this book.)

2. Organizing your **CAMP**:

➤ Number the following words in the order of importance to you:

_____ **C**ompetition

_____ **A**cclaim

_____ **M**oney

_____ **P**eople

3. Making use of negative statements:

➤ Compose a short paragraph to a friend explaining the drawbacks and disadvantages of one of your hobbies or interests. Try to convince your friend not to be involved in the activity. Use a multitude of apostrophe *Ts* and negative statements. An example of "garbage in, garbage out, goodness in, goodness out" is found on page four of *Acronyms Building Character.*

_____

_____

_____

_____

_____

_____

_____

4. Transforming negative statements into positive statements:

➤ Now compose a short paragraph explaining that same hobby or interest without using apostrophe *Ts* and negativism. Attempt to build your friend's interest so he or she can develop confidence in the endeavor.

_____

_____

_____

_____

_____

_____

_____

• CHECK

"If you don't like something, change it, if you can't change it, change your attitude. Don't complain." —Maya Angelou

Would you like to meet your life's expectations of levity, legacy, and longevity? Are you able to have fun, do a lot for a lot of people, and hope to live a long time to accomplish those things? Do you agree that your first goal will be to unequivocally learn to develop the desire to change what needs to be changed in your life to meet these goals?

• CONFIDENCE

"Your vision will become clear only when you can look into your own heart. Who looks outside, dreams; who looks inside, awakens."—Carl Jung

May I suggest that your goal for this chapter be a "Desire to Change?" Without a desire to change, the word *change* is simply a space containing six letters of wasted ink. You probably have wasted your time opening this book if you still lack a desire to change some ingredients of your existence. I certainly hope you will seek this journey of change to discover a more fulfilling and happy life. List your goal(s) on the following forms and periodically check on your progress to help fulfill your "life's expectations."

ASSESSING GOALS*

List your goal(s) and assign a number from 0 to 10 (10 being high) to each consideration of the goals setting process.

GOALS ➤➤➤➤➤➤➤➤➤ _____   _____
	(Primary Goal)	(Secondary Goal)
1. Level of need/passion	____	____
2. Level of desire to sacrifice	____	____
3. Level of research/planning	____	____
4. Level of action/skills	____	____
5. Ability to accept change	____	____
6. Ability to endure criticism	____	____
7. Available resources/assistance	____	____
8. Available time/energy	____	____
9. History of patience	____	____
10. History of commitment	____	____

Probability Index Total   ____   ____

Probability Index Scoring

90–100 . . . . . . Celebrate!	40–49 . . . . . . Should you reassess your goal?
80–89 . . . . Go for it!	30–39 . . . . . . Was your addition correct?
70–79 . . . . Have you analyzed obstacles?	20–29 . . . . . . Did you follow the directions?
60–69 . . . . Can you change anything?	10–19 . . . . . . Is it time for a reality check?
50–59 . . . . Is it worth the risk?	0–9 . . . . . . Possibly seek professional help?

*Greatness Only Awaits Labor…Staaaaaaaaaart!

_____

(CHAPTER TITLE)

_____

(GOAL/VISION/DREAM)

There is a need because:

_____

_____

The change, sacrifices and criticism that need to be addressed are:

_____

_____

_____

The assistance and resources that need to be procured are:

_____

_____

The history of patience and commitment has been:

_____

_____

In order to reach the goal I will:

_____

_____

_____

_____

_____

_____

_____

The beginning timeline is:

Set Goals	Planning	Implement	Completion?	Completed!
___/___/_____	___/___/_____	___/___/_____	___/___/_____	___/___/_____

The celebration plans are:

_____

_____

_____

(CHAPTER TITLE)

_____

(GOAL/VISION/DREAM)

There is a need because:

_____

_____

The change, sacrifices and criticism that need to be addressed are:

_____

_____

_____

The assistance and resources that need to be procured are:

_____

_____

The history of patience and commitment has been:

_____

_____

In order to reach the goal I will:

_____

_____

_____

_____

_____

_____

_____

The beginning timeline is:

Set Goals	Planning	Implement	Completion?	Completed!
___/___/____	___/___/____	___/___/____	___/___/____	___/___/____

The celebration plans are:

_____

_____

Indicate the acronyms that will help you achieve your goals.

ACCEPTANCE	All Circumstances Can Eventually Produce Truth And Negate Certain Excuses
ADAPT	Always Developing Attitudes Providing Trust
ASK	Always Seek Knowledge
BORED	Bring On Recreation Every Day
BOREDOM	Bring On Relationships Ending Doldrums Over Me
CAN	Character Advances Nobility
CONFIDENCE	Changing Our Negative Fears Invites Delightful Experiences Never Considered Easy
DESIRE	Does Everyone Strive In Reaching Excellence
FACT	Finding Actual Circumstances True
FAMILY	Friends Always Manage Inspirational Love Ya know
FREE	Feel Renewed Empowerment Everyday
FUN	Forget Unnecessary Nonsense
GIFT	Good Intentions For Things
GO	Great Opportunity
GOALS	Goodness Only Awaits Labor—Start
HABITS	Harmful Actions Blindly Injuring Thoughts'n Self
HAPPY	Have All' the Pleasure'n Peace Y'want
HEALTH	Hopefully Everyone Accesses Life's Trip Happily
HELP	Hurry Everyone Loves Progress
HOPE	Harnessing Optimism Produces Empowerment
HUMOR	Help Undo My Ordinary Response
IDIOTS	Individual's Debilitating Ideas Offends Team
LAUGH	Levity Always Underscores Good Habits
LIFE	Love Is For Everyone
NEED	Notice Everyone's Esteem Develop
NEGATIVE	Never Enjoy Goodness Always Treat Individuals Very Egotistically
PEACE	Practicing Effective Attitudes Calms Everyone
PLEASURE	Pain Leaves Eventually And Serenity Unfolds Refreshing Everyone
POSITIVE	Please Offer Sincere Insights To Instill Values Effectively
PROGRESS	People Reform Or Garner Refinement Establishing Some Success
PURPOSE	Producing Ultimate Rewards Produces Our Self-respect Effectively
SECRET	Sure Everyone Carefully Reserves Elaborate Truths
SOUL	Source Of Unconditional Love
STRESS	Sure Tough Regularly Exercising Self Sacrifice
SUCCESS	Seek Understanding Carefully Character Eventually Sows Satisfaction
TALENT	To Achieve, Latent Energy Needs Training
VISION	Very Intense Statement Indicating Objectives Necessary
WANT	Wishes Always Need Time
YET	Yes Eventually'n Time

CHANGE

WWW.CHARACTERCONSTRUCTIONCOMPANY.COM

ACROSS

4 Feel Renewed Empowerment Everyday

8 Goodness Only Awaits Labor Start

9 Great Opportunity

10 Source Of Unconditional Love

12 Sure Everyone Carefully Reserves Elaborate Truths

13 Good Intentions For Things

15 Individual's Debilitating Ideas Offends Teams

17 Harnessing Optimism Produces Empowerment

18 Notice Everyone's Esteem Develop

19 Changing Our Negative Fears Invites Delightful Experiences Never Considered Easy

24 Practicing Effective Attitudes Calms Everyone

26 Bring On Recreation Every Day

27 Sure Tough Regularly Exercising Self Sacrifice

28 Always Seek Knowledge

32 Have All the Peace'n Pleasure Y' want

34 To Achieve Latent Energy Needs Training

35 Help Undo My Ordinary Response

36 Wishes Always Need Time

38 Pain Leaves Eventually And Serenity Unfolds Refreshing Everyone

DOWN

1 Hopefully Everyone Accesses Life's Trip Happily

2 All Circumstances Can Eventually Produce Truth And Negate Certain Excuses

3 Never Enjoy Goodness Always Treat Individuals Very Egotistically

5 Please Offer Sincere Insights To Instill Values Effectively

6 People Reform Or Garner Refinement Establishing Some Success

7 Very Intense Statement Indicating Objectives Necessary

11 Love Is For Everyone

14 Bring On Relationships Ending Doldrums Over Me

16 Seek Understanding Carefully Character Eventually Sows Satisfaction

20 Find Actual Circumstances True

21 Levity Always Underscores Good Habits

22 Always Developing Attitudes Providing Trust

23 Harmful Actions Blindly Injuring Thoughts'n Self

24 Producing Ultimate Rewards Produces Our Self-respect Effectively

25 Hurry Everyone Loves Progress

29 Friends Always Manage Inspirational Love Ya know

30 Does Everyone Strive In Reaching Excellence

31 Forget Unnecessary Nonsense

33 Yes Eventually'n Time

37 Character Advances Nobility

CHANGE

Find the words in the grid. When you are done, the unused letters in the grid will spell out a hidden message. Pick them out from left to right, top line to bottom line. Words can go horizontally, vertically and diagonally in all eight directions.

```
S T A L E N T T H E F I R S H T S T
E O P I S F R E E H E L P T A F D E
S I U A S K R E T O C H L T H A U N
T G E L J I S L G Z Y A P B L O G N
E T H R D E S B X L E A R Y O O P T
R R L I X C E T M H D X L K S R M E
C L O C Z N C C S A C I Q T C E E Y
E T A P Q A C A M T N R T V N M D
S N T W H T U F N A I E N I B N P H
Y B W K W P S Q F O S B T M O C U U
E E L M P E A C E S I A A D R Y R M
E R T T H C S L A O G S H E D P O
N F I T K C R W T E T Y I K D E O R
L T I S K A H L N N K P F V O E S K
T R L L E R U S A E L P T V M N E R
H G U A L D B W F Y L A Y R P T N C
E C N E D I F N O C L H W L M H T B
H P O S I T I V E W P R O G R E S S
```

ACCEPTANCE	FREE	HUMOR	PURPOSE
ADAPT	FUN	IDIOTS	SECRET
ASK	GIFT	LAUGH	SOUL
BORED	GO	LIFE	STRESS
BOREDOM	GOALS	NEED	SUCCESS
CAN	HABITS	NEGATIVE	TALENT
CONFIDENCE	HAPPY	PEACE	VISION
DESIRE	HEALTH	PLEASURE	WANT
FACT	HELP	POSITIVE	YET
FAMILY	HOPE	PROGRESS	

HONESTY
Helping Others Notice Each Situation Truthfully

- ## CONNECT
  ### Learning how to be honest with yourself

  Many people _____ (Wickedness Only Results'n Resentment Y'know) and _____ (Carefully Object Making People Listen Aggravates Individuals Needlessly) about the _____ (Depicting Integrity Granting Nobility In Thy Years) and _____ (Allowing Change Towards Improvement Offers Needed Success) of others. You will always need to _____ (To Rely Upon Someone's Tenacity) what you are saying even if others _____ (To Respect Yourself) to _____ (Losers Intentionally Exaggerate), _____ (Fact Intentionally Bent) or _____ (Believable Lies Undermine Faith Forever) you by altering a _____ (Finding Actual Circumstances True) of a situation.

- ## CHALLENGE
  ### Learning to disseminate only the information that is required to ensure honesty

  1. Deciding what information to divulge (check one):

  ➢ While visiting your doctor you should answer:
     - ____ a. all of the questions regarding the diagnosis of your ailment.
     - ____ b. some of the questions you are asked during the diagnosis of your ailment.
     - ____ c. most of the questions you are asked during the diagnosis of your ailment.

  2. How to accept honest compliments (check one):

  ➢ When you are offered a compliment, which might be a partial diagnosis of your character, you should:
     - ____ a. argue.
     - ____ b. display appreciation.
     - ____ c. say nothing.

  3. How to endure dishonesty (check one):

  ➢ If you know someone is being dishonest you should:
     - ____ a. try to do what they say so you have someone to blame.
     - ____ b. possibly seek clarification, display your disbelief, and ensure the truth is clearly known.
     - ____ c. tell them that Losers Intentionally Exaggerate and start a fist fight.

4. How to endure accusations of being dishonest (check one):

➢ If someone accuses you of lying, but you didn't lie you should:
    ____ a. ask for clarification of why they feel that way.
    ____ b. attempt to determine if they are correct.
    ____ c. politely tell them you are sorry they feel that way.
    ____ d. consider the source and try to forget about it.
    ____ e. possibly all of the above.
    ____ f. possibly all of the above.

5. Understanding whether total honesty is always the best policy (check one):

➢ You should always:
    ____ a. tell everything you know about the topic to everyone who will listen.
    ____ b. not be concerned about the feelings of others if they can't handle the truth.
    ____ c. let everyone know the information, they can decide if it's the truth.
    ____ d. possibly none of the above.
    ____ e. possibly none of the above.

6. Knowing when being dishonest might be acceptable (check one):

➢   Unless you are breaking rules or laws, you might consider it permissible to lie if:
    ____ a. someone might be physically harmed by revealing the truth.
    ____ b. someone might be emotionally harmed by revealing the truth.
    ____ c. you are trying to guard a mystery or secret such as the whereabouts of the tooth fairy.
    ____ d. all of the above.
    ____ e. all of the above.

7. Avoiding the "Hobin Rood" principle (check one):

➢ Being dishonest in business practices is acceptable if:
    ____ a. you can inflate prices and not get caught.
    ____ b. you can fool people about the value of a product or service.
    ____ c. you can avoid fulfilling agreements and promises without getting caught.
    ____ d. none of the above.
    ____ e. none of the above.

8. How to endure being called a liar (check one):

➢ If someone accuses you of lying, but you didn't lie you should:
    ____ a. consider the source.
    ____ b. consider the source.
    ____ c. consider the source.
    ____ d. all of the above.
    ____ e. all of the above.

• CHANNEL

Analyzing situations involving a variety of aspects of honesty

1. Deciding what information to divulge:

➤ Describe a situation where unnecessary conflicts occurred because more information was divulged than needed to be given. You might consider an incident when someone broke the confidence of another person to tell you information that you did not need to know.

_____

_____

_____

_____

_____

2. How to accept honest compliments:

➤ Relate a situation when you offered someone a compliment and they did not agree with the compliment.

_____

_____

_____

_____

_____

3. How to endure dishonesty:

➤ Explain a circumstance where a friend of yours was able to forgive someone for being less than truthful.

_____

_____

_____

_____

_____

4. How to endure accusations of being dishonest:

➤ Explain how you have been called a liar and you were able to respond in an appropriate manner.

_____

_____

_____

_____

5. Understanding if total honesty is always the best policy:

➤ Relate an incident when reserving all of the facts was the correct method of avoiding a conflict.

_____

_____

_____

_____

6. Knowing when being dishonest might be acceptable:

➤ Tell a story regarding the use of a fib or little white lie that was acceptable because it avoided a conflict.

_____

_____

_____

_____

7. Avoiding the "Hobin Rood" principle:

➤ Relate an incident or possibly a news report that depicts rich people robbing from the poor.

_____

_____

_____

_____

8. How to endure being called a liar:

➢ Explain what best helps you "live through" being mistakenly called a liar.

_____

_____

_____

_____

• CHECK

Can you be honest with yourself about what you need to be honest about?

• CONFIDENCE

"…always tell the truth. Then you'll never have to remember what you said last time."—**Mark Twain**

➢ Select one or two elements of honesty that you would like to improve upon in your life and assess them on the Assessing Goals form and the Goal/Vision/Dream form.

ASSESSING GOALS*

*List your goal(s) and assign a number from 0 to 10 (10 being high)
to each consideration of the goals setting process.*

GOALS ➤➤➤➤➤➤➤➤➤ _____   _____
(Primary Goal)   (Secondary Goal)

	(Primary Goal)	(Secondary Goal)
1. Level of need/passion	_____	_____
2. Level of desire to sacrifice	_____	_____
3. Level of research/planning	_____	_____
4. Level of action/skills	_____	_____
5. Ability to accept change	_____	_____
6. Ability to endure criticism	_____	_____
7. Available resources/assistance	_____	_____
8. Available time/energy	_____	_____
9. History of patience	_____	_____
10. History of commitment	_____	_____

Probability Index Total   _____   _____

Probability Index Scoring

90–100 . . . . . . Celebrate!	40–49 . . . . . . Should you reassess your goal?
80–89 . . . . Go for it!	30–39 . . . . . Was your addition correct?
70–79 . . . . Have you analyzed obstacles?	20–29 . . . . . . Did you follow the directions?
60–69 . . . . Can you change anything?	10–19 . . . . . . Is it time for a reality check?
50–59 . . . . Is it worth the risk?	0–9 . . . . . . Possibly seek professional help?

*Greatness Only Awaits Labor…Staaaaaaaaart!

_____

(CHAPTER TITLE)

_____

(GOAL/VISION/DREAM)

There is a need because:

_____
_____

The change, sacrifices and criticism that need to be addressed are:

_____
_____
_____

The assistance and resources that need to be procured are:

_____
_____

The history of patience and commitment has been:

_____
_____

In order to reach the goal I will:

_____
_____
_____
_____
_____
_____
_____

The beginning timeline is:

Set Goals	Planning	Implement	Completion?	Completed!
___/___/_____	___/___/_____	___/___/_____	___/___/_____	___/___/_____

The celebration plans are:

_____
_____

_____

(CHAPTER TITLE)

_____

(GOAL/VISION/DREAM)

There is a need because:

_____

_____

The change, sacrifices and criticism that need to be addressed are:

_____

_____

_____

The assistance and resources that need to be procured are:

_____

_____

The history of patience and commitment has been:

_____

_____

In order to reach the goal I will:

_____

_____

_____

_____

_____

_____

_____

The beginning timeline is:

Set Goals	Planning	Implement	Completion?	Completed!
___/___/____	___/___/____	___/___/____	___/___/____	___/___/____

The celebration plans are:

_____

_____

Indicate the acronyms that will help you achieve your goals.

ACTIONS	Allowing Change Toward Improvement Offers Needed Success
ANGER	Acclaiming Negative Garbage Eradicates Relationships
ARREST	A Required Reservation Employing Self-discipline Training
ASK	Always Seek Knowledge
BELIEVE	Bountiful Experiences Loved If Everyone Visualizes Eventualities
BEST	Beautiful Endeavors Seem Terrific
BLUFF	Believable Lies Undermine Faith Forever
COMPLAIN	Carefully Object— Making People Listen Aggravates Individuals Needlessly
DIGNITY	Depicting Integrity Granting Nobility In Thy Years
EGOS	Everybody Greedily Owns Some
EGOTIST	Everybody Gags On The Individual's Selfish Traits
FACT	Finding Actual Circumstances True
FAITH	Forget All Insecurities; Trust Hope
FEEL	Faith Eventually Elevates Love
FIB	Facts Intentionally Bent
FREEDOM	Forget Restrictions Enjoy Every Day's Opportunistic Moments
FUN	Forget Unnecessary Nonsense
GOALS	Greatness Only Awaits Labor—Staaaaaaaaaart
HELP	Hurry Everyone Loves Progress
HOPE	Harnessing Optimism Produces Empowerment
IDEA	Inspiration Deserves Everyone's Attention
IF	Initiate Fantasies
IMPROVE	Individuals Make Progress Rewarding Our Valiant Efforts
KIND	Keep It Nice Dear
LAW	Learn Allowable Ways
LIE	Losers Intentionally Exaggerate
LUCK	Languishing Using Current Knowledge
MAD	Meanness Always Destroys
PEACE	Practicing Effective Attitudes Calms Everyone
PROFITS	Providing Revenue Opportunities Fulfills Individual Tasks Successfully
REALITY	Recognizing Eventualities, Accepting Life's Inequities Teaches You
RELATIONSHIPS	Realizing Every Love, Attaining Truth In Our Negative Situations, Helps Individuals Produce Satisfaction
RESPOND	Respecting Every Statement People Offer Needs Diligence
RIGHT	Respecting Individuals Grants Honor Today
RUDE	Really Useless Defensive Endeavors

RULES	Regulating Us Leads Everyone to Success
SMILE	Sure Makes It Lots Easier
SORRY	Success Often Requires Rescinding Yourself
TEAM	Tolerance Empowers All Members
TRUST	Thoroughly Relying Upon Someone's Tenacity
WINNERS	We Interrupt Negativism Now Everyone Reaches Success
WORRY	Wickedness Only Result'n Resentment Y'know

HONESTY

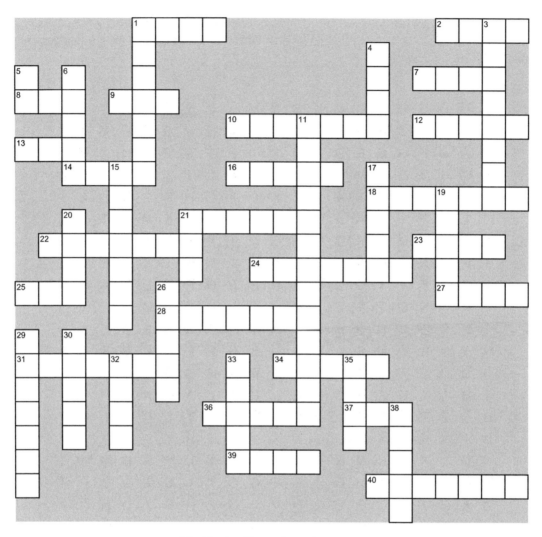

ACROSS

1 Beautiful Endeavors Seem Terrific
2 Languishing Using Current Knowledge
7 Tolerance Empowers All Members
8 Forget Unnecessary Nonsense
9 Facts Intentionally Bent
10 Individuals Make Progress Rewarding Our Valiant Efforts
12 Greatness Only Awaits Labor Start
13 Losers Intentionally Exaggerate
14 Really Useless Defensive Endeavors
16 Sure Makes It Lots Easier
18 Respecting Every Statement People Offer Needs Diligence
21 A Required Reservation Employing Self-discipline Training
22 We Interrupt Negativism Now Everyone Reaches Success
23 Finding Actual Circumstances True
24 Providing Revenue Opportunities Fulfills Individual Tasks Successfully
25 Meanness Always Destroys
27 Everybody Greedily Owns Some

28 Allowing Change Towards Improvement Offers Needed Success
31 Everybody Gags On The Individual's Selfish Traits
34 Respecting Individuals Grants Honor Today
36 Regulating Us Leads Everyone to Success
37 Learn Allowable Ways
39 Faith Eventually Elevates Love
40 Forget Restrictions Enjoy Every Day's Opportunistic Moments

DOWN

1 Bountiful Experiences Loved If Everyone Visualizes Eventualities
3 Carefully Object Making People Listen Aggravates Individuals Needlessly
4 Harnessing Optimism Produces Empowerment
5 Initiate Fantasies
6 Acclaiming Negative Garbage Eradicates Relationships

11 Realizing Every Love, Attaining Truth In Our Negative Situations, Helps Individuals Produce Satisfaction
15 Depicting Integrity Granting Nobility In Thy Years
17 Thoroughly Relying Upon Someone's Tenacity
19 Practicing Effective Attitudes Calms Everyone
20 Keep It Nice Dear
21 Always Seek Knowledge
26 Forget All Insecurities; Trust Hope
29 Recognizing Eventualities, Accepting Life's Inequities Teaches You
30 Success Often Requires Rescinding Yourself
32 Inspiration Deserves Everyone's Attention
33 Believable Lies Undermine Faith Forever
35 Hurry Everyone Loves Progress
38 Wickedness Only Results'n Resentment Y'know

HONESTY

Find the words in the grid. When you are done, the unused letters in the grid will spell out a hidden message. Pick them out from left to right, top line to bottom line. Words can go horizontally, vertically and diagonally in all eight directions.

```
L O D S E L U C K S R M A E T S I N T E N
T I O N I N A L L N Y E E E V O R P M I X
F A G F O G E R A O T I E T S V B R X H Z
A W J J B P M N F I L T W L T T J Q A N N
I A D K T M S M R T K C A L H B S S D S F
T L Y T I L A E R C Y O P G G E M R T J K
H F S F M V K G R A G M I P Y L I E P L L
T H P K T O N V F R F R T R R I L N E Q G
Y J I F T T D Q R A N P R N R E E N A X M
T K H N Q T P E T N C O X H Q V M I C Y V
I P S W C R G B E S W T M K W E R W E B V
N T N K O N S D B R U L N F F U L B R S B
G D O F A O Y F L X F R N I C D J V O B L
I B I T G Z E B H E L P T L A N N R H T Z
D T T E Z E E L N A R R E S T L R I L B T
S I A R L S M R U K T Y C T D Y P L K W X
K D L X T R M N F Y R T K Y L P K M M W T
M E E C D H U C J F E G O T I S T Q O P T
Q A R J T G O L Q N M L G Z H H Z D H C K
L Z D L B I F P E X N G F F R C W R U D E
J D V P M K G L E S V T F Z Q D T G F H M
```

ACTIONS	EGOS	HELP	MAD	RESPOND
ANGER	EGOTIST	HOPE	PEACE	RIGHT
ARREST	FACT	IDEA	PROFITS	RUDE
ASK	FAITH	IF	SMILE	RULES
BELIEVE	FEEL	IMPROVE	SORRY	WINNERS
BEST	FIB	KIND	TEAM	WORRY
BLUFF	FREEDOM	LAW	TRUST	
COMPLAIN	FUN	LIE	REALITY	
DIGNITY	GOALS	LUCK	RELATIONSHIPS	

ATTITUDE

All Terrific Thoughts Incorporate The Unrelenting Desire for Excellence

• CONNECT

Learning to respond in an appropriate manner

If we _____ (**C**ourage **A**lways **R**esonates **E**ndearingly) how we _____ (**A**lways **C**arefully **T**read) by remaining _____ (**P**lease **O**ffer **S**incere **I**nsights **T**o **I**nstill **V**alues **E**ffectively), we can avoid becoming an _____ **E**verybody **G**ags **O**n The **I**ndividual's **S**elfish **T**raits) and a _____ (**B**rashness **U**ltimately **L**essens **L**oving **Y**ou) in the eyes of others by displaying an attitude full of _____ (**H**urtful **A**ttitudes **T**est **E**veryone). _____ (**H**elp **E**veryone **R**egardless **O**f **E**ncountering **S**tress) display _____ (**F**orget **A**ll **I**nsecurities **T**rust **H**ope) when they don't allow people to _____ (**T**o **E**njoy **A**buse **S**ignifies **E**vil) and _____ (**H**urt **A**lways **R**esults **A**s **S**arcasm **S**oars) others. Heroes _____ (**T**o **R**espect **Y**ourself) to develop a _____ (**C**ontrol **A**ll **N**egativism; **D**evelop **O**ptimism) _____ (**A**ll **T**errific **T**houghts **I**ncorporate **T**he **U**nrelenting **D**esire for **E**xcellence) and remove _____ (**F**reezes **E**very **A**ction…**R**econsider) from every _____ (**R**espect **E**very **S**tatement **P**eople **O**ffer; **N**ever **S**eem **E**gotistical).

• CHALLENGE

Understanding that inappropriate reactions are what usually causes the most conflicts

1. Recognizing positive role models:

➢ List three people who have influenced you by being positive individuals (initials will be fine).

_____

_____

_____

23

➤ List three people who have been role models of negativism that you do not want to emulate or copy (initials will be fine).

_____

_____

_____

2. Learning to respond in a positive manner:

➤ Add positive words and negative words similar to the words in the following example:

_____ Faith	**F**	Fear _____
_____ Opportunity	**O**	Obligation _____
_____ Care	**C**	Confrontation _____
_____ Understanding	**U**	Useless _____
_____ Success	**S**	Screaming _____

3. Being able to recognize negativity that develops into harassment:

➤ The three most common forms of harassment are verbal, physical, and visual. Circle the six underlined words in the following sentence that indicate the presence of harassment.

You are being harassed if you feel <u>disturbed</u>, <u>tormented</u>, and/or <u>pestered</u> on a persistent basis by what you <u>hear</u>, <u>feel</u>, and/or <u>see</u>.

4. Knowing when to seek assistance:

➤ You know it is time to seek assistance from someone you can trust if you feel…
this one's **really** easy…(check one):

_____ a. Disturbed, tormented, and/or pestered by what you hear, feel, and/or see.

5. Understanding the importance of stating facts and avoiding personal attacks:

➤ If you need to be criticized, how would you like the message delivered? (check one)

_____ a. "Don't you know what you're supposed to do?"
_____ b. "What you need to know for the future is…"
_____ c. "It's just in your nature because you aren't very smart."
_____ d. none of the above.
_____ e. all of the above.

6. Understanding the risks of asking questions regarding right and wrong:

➤ If you are being criticized by someone regarding their perception of right and wrong, would it be best for that person to say (check one):

        _____ a. "Don't you know right from wrong?"
        _____ b. "What you did wrong was…"
        _____ c. "Don't you think what I told you was important?"
        _____ d. none of the above.
        _____ e. all of the above.

7. How to achieve success while tolerating someone's less than desirable attitude:

➤ Many times in order to achieve success we must learn to tolerate someone who has a (check all of the appropriate answers):

        _____ a. lazy attitude.
        _____ b. negative attitude.
        _____ c. non committal attitude.
        _____ d. poisonous attitude.
        _____ e. all of the above.

• CHANNEL

Analyzing your experience of positive influence

1. Recognizing positive role models:

➤ List three people who have influenced you by being positive and cooperative (initials are fine).

PEOPLE	INFLUENCE
_____	_____
_____	_____
_____	_____

➤ List three people you have influenced to be positive and cooperative (initials are fine).

PEOPLE	INFLUENCE
_____	_____
_____	_____
_____	_____

2. Learning to respond in a positive manner:

➤ Each line contains a positive response and a negative response.
Place a plus (+) by the statements you would like to hear and say more often.
Place a minus (−) by the statements you would like to hear and say less often.

____ "I don't know why you..."   ____ "Can I help you figure out..."

____ "I sure appreciate your..."   ____ "I don't like the way you..."

____ "What if we redirect it towards..."   ____ "I have a bone to pick with you..."

____ "You always need help determining..."   ____ "Have you thought about..."

____ "You should have known that..."   ____ "Next time what if we consider..."

____ "It's in your nature that you..."   ____ "You'll be happier if..."

____ "We need to talk about..."   ____ "We need to talk..."

____ "Where are you with this so far..."   ____ "Don't you know that..."

____ "Why did you ever think that...   ____ "What have you learned from this..."

____ "You don't understand me..."   ____ "I'll try to be more clear about..."

____ "What we've always done is..."   ____ "So far we've found what works best is..."

____ "You are wrong because..."   ____ "I understand, have you considered..."

____ "There you go again; I told you..."   ____ "Can you help me with some ideas..."

____ "Which one of you messed it up..."   ____ "Who has a better idea of how to..."

____ "See me..."   ____ "Please see me about..."

____ "My impression of what you said..."   ____ "You said that..."

____ "You might avoid a conflict if..."   ____ "I'll get mad if..."

(Add several additional statements)

"_____"   "_____"

"_____"   "_____"

"_____"   "_____"

"_____"   "_____"

➤ Match the letter from the second column to the more appropriate comment in the first column.

1. ___ "Can I explain my opinion about…"   A. "You said that…"

2. ___ "Have you thought about…"   B. "Don't you know that…?"

3. ___ "I certainly appreciate your idea…"   C. "I know we disagree; you're wrong…"

4. ___ "You'll probably be happier if…"   D. "See me."

5. ___ "My impression of what you said was…"   E. "I don't appreciate the way you…"

6. ___ "I understand; have you considered…"   F. "I'll get mad if…"

7. ___ "Please see me about…"   G. "I have a bone to pick with you…"

8. ___ "Who has a better idea how to…"   H. "Who messed up the…?"

9. ___ "What we have found that works is…"   I. "I don't know why you…"

10. ___ "What have you learned from…"   J. "What we've always done is…

➤ List and match three additional positive and negative statements similar to the above.

" _____ " " _____ "

" _____ " " _____ "

" _____ " " _____ "

➤ Copy and complete a positive and corresponding negative statement from the above listings.

POSITIVE	NEGATIVE
Sample—"Can I help you figure out how… to correctly complete that project?	*Sample*—"I don't know why you keep doing that wrong. If you weren't such an idiot you would know better"

_____   _____

_____   _____

_____   _____

_____   _____

_____   _____

3. Being able to recognize an attitude that displays harassment (check one in each section):

➤ Is visual harassment taking place if someone displays suggestive or inappropriate printed words, pictures, cartoons, etc., that disturb you?

>   Yes _____

➤ Is verbal harassment occurring if someone pesters you by making inappropriate comments about your physical appearance, background, spiritual beliefs, ethnicity, name, social standing, gender, disability, age, weight, etc?

>   Yes _____

➤ Is physical harassment taking place if someone torments you by forcibly blocking your access to freely move about?

>   Yes _____

➤ Is physical harassment taking place if someone displays an inappropriate level of affection or physically threatens you?

>   Yes _____

➤ If any of the above situations occur, your first response should be to:

>   _____ a. accept it.
>   _____ b. make it very clear that you disapprove.
>   _____ c. ignore it.
>   _____ d. feel guilty.

➤ If an uncomfortable situation continues after you display your disapproval you should:

>   _____ a. accept it.
>   _____ b. report the situation.
>   _____ c. attempt to forget about it.
>   _____ d. feel guilty.

➤ If you are dissatisfied with the reaction and/or actions of the person to whom you report the situation you should:

>   _____ a. report to a higher authority.
>   _____ b. attempt to forget about it.
>   _____ c. blame yourself.
>   _____ d. feel guilty.

➤ After reporting it to a higher authority, if you are dissatisfied with their reaction and/or actions you should:

>   _____ a. report to a higher authority.
>   _____ b. attempt to forget about it.
>   _____ c. blame yourself.
>   _____ d. feel guilty.

➤ If you are dissatisfied with the reaction and/or actions of the person to whom you attempted to report the situation you should:

       _____ a. seek help from a different source.
       _____ b. attempt to forget about it.
       _____ c. blame yourself.
       _____ d. feel guilty.

4. Knowing when to seek assistance:

On many occasions there is a fine line between sincere compliments, pestering, appropriate comments, tormenting remarks, welcomed humor, disturbing jokes, constructive criticism, bullying, fun, teasing, helping, and harassing. There is always a danger of offending others by criticizing, displaying affection, making compliments, and telling jokes. The spirit and intent of statements and actions should always be carefully considered to hopefully avoid offending others.

➤ Each line contains a positive remark and a negative remark.
Place a plus (+) by the statements you would like to hear and say more often.
Place a minus (–) by the statements you would like to hear and say less often.

_____ "You look really sharp and you work that way…"   _____ "Are you as dumb as you look…?"

_____ "Maybe you act stupid because your name is…"   _____ "Your family must be proud…"

_____ "That outfit really shows off your body…"   _____ "You look great in that outfit…"

_____ "If you need some help I'll…"   _____ "If you don't…I'm going to…"

_____ "You act like the stupid person that…"   _____ "I have respect for you because…"

_____ "If you don't tell anybody, I'll make an offer…"   _____ "You're great because…"

_____ "I'll hit you if you don't do what I tell you…"   _____ "I'll be happy to help you with…."

_____ "Did you see that cartoon in the newspaper…?"   _____ "Don't tell I said to look at…"

(Add several more)

_____ "_____"   _____ "_____"

_____ "_____"   _____ "_____"

_____ "_____"   _____ "_____"

_____ "_____"   _____ "_____"

5. Understanding the importance of stating appropriate facts while avoiding personal attacks:

➤ Each line contains a positive response and a negative response.
Place a plus (+) by the statements you would like to hear and say more often.
Place a minus (−) by the statements you would hope to hear and say less often.

___ "Your mind seems to be someplace else..."   ___ "Don't you think what I'm saying is...?"

___ "Don't you know you aren't supposed to...?"   ___ "What you did was incorrect because..."

___ "I appreciate your questions because..."   ___ "Your question is stupid because..."

___ "If you were smart you would have known..."   ___ "In the future you might consider..."

___ "You have been informed the policy is..."   ___ "Don't you know the policy is...?"

___ "_____"   ___ "_____"

___ "_____"   ___ "_____"

6. Understanding the risk of asking questions in some situations:

➤ Each line contains a positive response and a negative response.
Place a plus (+) by the statements you would like to hear and say more often.
Place a minus (–) by the statements you would hope to hear and say less often

___ "Haven't I told you about that enough...?"   ___ "Let me remind you again that..."

___ "Don't you pay attention, because you don't...?"   ___ "Try to concentrate on..."

___ "Don't you think what I'm saying is important...?"   ___ "The important facts are..."

___ "Is the rumor I heard about you that...?"   ___ "I hope you feel that..."

___ "Don't you care about the fact that...?"   ___ "You'll care more if..."

(Add several more combinations)

___ "_____"   ___ "_____"

___ "_____"   ___ "_____"

___ "_____"   ___ "_____"

7. How to achieve success while tolerating someone's poisonous attitude (check correct answer(s) in each section):

➤ A person with a poisonous attitude is usually attempting to:

     ___ a. receive attention.

     ___ b. be inconspicuous.

     ___ c. share warm feelings.

     ___ d. help others.

     ___ e. all of the above.

     ___ f. none of the above.

➢ A person with a poisonous attitude is usually trying to:

    _____ a. gain power.
    _____ b. help people.
    _____ c. not be noticed.
    _____ d. learn how to improve.
    _____ e. all of the above.
    _____ f. none of the above.

➢ Dealing with a person with a poisonous attitude is usually:

    _____ a. very easy.
    _____ b. very easy to forget.
    _____ c. very challenging.
    _____ d. very comforting.
    _____ e. all of the above.
    _____ f. none of the above.

➢ An effective method of dealing with a person possessing a poisonous attitude is to:

    _____ a. tactfully attempt to discover the source of their anger and help them reconcile it.
    _____ b. learn methods of functioning in spite of their power-hungry attitude.
    _____ c. provide them a level of power commensurate with their abilities.
    _____ d. seek assistance in assessing the source of their anger.
    _____ e. help them procure counseling for managing their attitude.
    _____ f. attempt to remove yourself from their influence.
    _____ g. attempt to remove them from influencing you.
    _____ h. attempt to remove them from influencing others.
    _____ i. possibly all of the above.

➢ Explain what you have learned to help you get along with people who possess negative attitudes.

_____

_____

_____

_____

• CHECK

"It's so hard when I have to and so easy when I want to." — Anne Gottlier

• CONFIDENCE

"We may not be able to direct the wind; however, we can adjust our sails." — Buddha

➢ List one or two goals regarding your attitude on the following forms

ASSESSING GOALS*

*List your goal(s) and assign a number from 0 to 10 (10 being high)
to each consideration of the goals setting process.*

GOALS ➤➤➤➤➤➤➤➤➤ _____   _____
(Primary Goal)   (Secondary Goal)

	(Primary Goal)	(Secondary Goal)
1. Level of need/passion	_____	_____
2. Level of desire to sacrifice	_____	_____
3. Level of research/planning	_____	_____
4. Level of action/skills	_____	_____
5. Ability to accept change	_____	_____
6. Ability to endure criticism	_____	_____
7. Available resources/assistance	_____	_____
8. Available time/energy	_____	_____
9. History of patience	_____	_____
10. History of commitment	_____	_____

Probability Index Total   _____   _____

Probability Index Scoring

90–100 . . . . . . Celebrate!   40–49 . . . . . . Should you reassess your goal?
80–89 . . . . Go for it!   30–39 . . . . . . Was your addition correct?
70–79 . . . . Have you analyzed obstacles?   20–29 . . . . . . Did you follow the directions?
60–69 . . . . Can you change anything?   10–19 . . . . . . Is it time for a reality check?
50–59 . . . . Is it worth the risk?   0–9 . . . . . . Possibly seek professional help?

*Greatness Only Awaits Labor…Staaaaaaaaaart!

_____

(CHAPTER TITLE)

_____

(GOAL/VISION/DREAM)

There is a need because:

_____

_____

The change, sacrifices and criticism that need to be addressed are:

_____

_____

_____

The assistance and resources that need to be procured are:

_____

_____

The history of patience and commitment has been:

_____

_____

In order to reach the goal I will:

_____

_____

_____

_____

_____

_____

_____

The beginning timeline is:

Set Goals	Planning	Implement	Completion?	Completed!
___/___/_____	___/___/_____	___/___/_____	___/___/_____	___/___/_____

The celebration plans are:

_____

_____

_____

(CHAPTER TITLE)

_____

(GOAL/VISION/DREAM)

There is a need because:

_____

_____

The change, sacrifices and criticism that need to be addressed are:

_____

_____

_____

The assistance and resources that need to be procured are:

_____

_____

The history of patience and commitment has been:

_____

_____

In order to reach the goal I will:

_____

_____

_____

_____

_____

_____

_____

The beginning timeline is:

Set Goals	Planning	Implement	Completion?	Completed!
___/___/_____	___/___/_____	___/___/_____	___/___/_____	___/___/_____

The celebration plans are:

_____

_____

Indicate the acronyms that will help you achieve your goals.

ACCEPT	All Circumstances Can Eventually Produce Truth
ACT	Always Carefully Tread
BULLY	Brashness Ultimately Lessens Loving You
CAN DO	Control All Negativism; Develop Optimism
CARE	Courage Always Resonates Endearingly
EGOTIST	Everybody Gags On The Individual's Selfish Traits
FAITH	Forget All Insecurities; Trust Hope
FEAR	Freezes Every Action; Reconsider
FOCUS	Faith, Opportunity, Care, Understanding, Success, Fear, Obligation, Confrontation, Useless, Screaming
FUN	Forget Unnecessary Nonsense
GREAT	Golden Rule Elevates All Teams
HATE	Hurtful Attitudes Test Everyone
HEROES	Help Everyone Regardless of Encountering Stress
HONESTY	Helping Others Notice Every Situation Truthfully
LOYALTY	Life Offers You All Levels, Trust Yours
NEGATIVE	Never Enjoy Goodness; Always Treat Individuals Very Egotistically
POSITIVE	Please Offer Sincere Insights To Instill Values Effectively
REALITIES	Recognizing Eventualities, Accepting Life's Inequities Teaches You
RESPONSE	Respect Every Statement People Offer Never Seem Egotistical
SMILE	Sure Makes It Lots Easier
SUCCESS	Seek Understanding Carefully; Character Eventually Sows Satisfaction
TEASE	To Enjoy Abuse Signifies Evil
TEST	To Evaluate Student's Teacher
THANKS	To Honestly Acknowledge Noble Kindness Shown
TRY	To Respect Yourself
WORRIES	Wickedness Only Results'n Resentment In Every Situation
YELL	You Eventually Lose Love

ATTITUDE

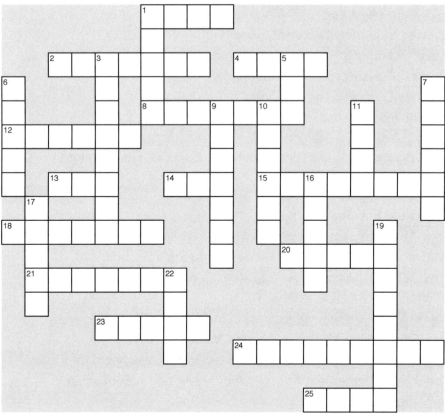

www.CharacterConstructionCompany.com

ACROSS

1 Freezes Every Action Reconsider

2 Wickedness Only Results'n Resentment In Every Situation

4 Hurtful Attitudes Test Everyone

8 Helping Others Notice Every Situation Truthfully

12 All Circumstances Can Eventually Produce Truth

13 Forget Unnecessary Nonsense

14 Always Carefully Tread

15 Never Enjoy Goodness Always Treat Individuals Very Egotistically

18 Seek Understanding Carefully Character Eventually Sows Satisfaction

20 Control All Negativism Develop Optimism

21 Life Offers You All Levels, Trust Yours

23 Sure Makes It Lots Easier

24 Recognizing Eventualities, Accepting Life's Inequities Teaches Individuals Everlasting Structure

25 Courage Always Resonates Endearingly

DOWN

1 Forget All Insecurities Trust Hope

3 Respect Every Statement People Offer Never Seem Egotistical

5 To Respect Yourself

6 To Enjoy Abuse Signifies Evil

7 Help Everyone Regardless Of Encountering Stress

9 Everybody Gags On The Individual's Selfish Traits

10 To Honestly Acknowledge Noble Kindness Shown

11 To Evaluate Student's Teacher

16 Golden Rule Elevates All Teams

17 Brashness Ultimately Lessens Loving You

19 Please Off Sincere Insights To Instill Values Effectively

22 You Eventually Lose Love

ATTITUDE

Find the words in the grid. When you are done, the unused letters in the grid will spell out a hidden message. Pick them out from left to right, top line to bottom line. Words can go horizontally, vertically and diagonally in all eight directions.

```
S T S T A N D T U P A N D Y E L
L P E W E C A N H A I L E D T H
I E I T L E A D N E L K C L E O
X C T L R K P N B H R K A L A N
M C I G X X M E D D X O R E S E
R A L R B L E L V O F J E Y E S
B Z A Y H G O S E I K Y H S M T
N N E F O Y Y S U T T L R H V Y
U R R T A T N T S C Y I R T T Z
F D I L G O W E T L C Z S L Q T
J S T W P T I J P T C E F O C Z
T Y X S E R M J V W H H S A P G
Y B E S R B U L L Y C T C S N F
G R T O L A D V F V C H T I A F
K N W H A T E P S K N A H T R R
P S M I L E K F E V I T A G E N
```

ACCEPT	FUN	RESPONSES
ACT	GREAT	SMILE
BULLY	HATE	SUCCESS
CANDO	HEROES	TEASE
CARE	HONESTY	TEST
EGOTIST	LOYALTY	THANKS
FAITH	NEGATIVE	TRY
FEAR	POSITIVE	WORRIES
FOCUS	REALITIES	YELL

RESPECT

Recognizing Everyone's Strengths
Produces Exceptional Caring Teams

- ## CONNECT

Expanding your concept from "Me" to "We"

Displaying _____ (**K**eep **I**ntentions **N**ice **D**e-escalate **N**egative **E**vents'n

Situations **S**wiftly) to others by being _____ (**N**ever **I**nsult **C**ompliment **E**veryone) will

_____ (**H**urry, **E**veryone **L**oves **P**rogress) individuals avoid becoming _____

(**E**verybody **G**ags **O**n **T**he **I**ndividual's **S**elfish **T**raits). People will then be able to receive the

_____ (**R**ealizing **E**veryone's **W**ork **A**ssures **R**ecognition **D**eserved) of having their

_____ (**D**esire **R**eflects **E**ventual **A**chievements **M**agically **S**ecured) come true and

reap _____ (**S**eek **U**nderstanding **C**arefully **C**haracter **E**ventually **S**ows **S**atisfaction) by

receiving _____ (**R**ecognizing **E**veryone's **S**trengths, **P**roduces **E**xceptional **C**aring **T**eams).

- ## CHALLENGE

How can we best remember to consider the wants and needs of others?

1. Avoiding placing blame:

➤ Check the most effective method of avoiding blame while enhancing relationships:

       ___ a. Forget about the situation; pretend it didn't happen.
       ___ b. Avoid discussing it; it might ruin the person's self-image.
       ___ c. State the facts of the situation and what should be done in the future.
       ___ d. All of the above.
       ___ e. None of the above.

2. Circumventing inappropriate reactions (check one):

➤ If you know that bringing up a topic from the past will create conflict you should:

       ___ a. Mention the topic often to instill a perpetual feeling of guilt, thus creating a reason to argue.
       ___ b. Forget about it; never bring it up. It will degrade the person's self-esteem.
       ___ c. Diplomatically state the facts of the situation, learning what to avoid in the future.
       ___ d. All of the above.
       ___ e. None of the above.

3. Keeping away from displaying selfishness (check one):

➤ To think of others first is always a major challenge. Which statement would you like to hear from others?

      ____ a. "Me and my friends think that you should…"
      ____ b. "Have you considered that a different direction might be best for you because…?"
      ____ c. "What will make me happy about how you are planning to do that is…"
      ____ d. All of the above.
      ____ e. None of the above.

4. Steering clear of being insulted (check one):

➤ If you are aware of people who perpetually insult you in an attempt to inflate their egos, you should probably:

      ____ a. Avoid their influence if possible.
      ____ b. State the facts of how you are interpreting their comments.
      ____ c. Hand them one of these books and encourage them to use it.
      ____ d. All of the above.
      ____ e. All of the above.

5. Avoiding insulting others (check one):

➤ Insulting others is usually an attempt to bolster our egos or a reaction to counteract an insult directed at us. The best chance of avoiding being involved in an insult would be to:

      ____ a. Live alone on a deserted island, so you won't be insulted, unless you talk to yourself.
      ____ b. Be KWIK and Kill With Instant Kindness.
      ____ c. Live alone in a cave, especially if you like loincloths.
      ____ d. Possibly all of the above.
      ____ e. None of the above.

• CHANNEL

Place a plus (+) on the left side of the statements you feel are important for displaying respect. Place a minus (−) on the left side of the statements you feel are not important for displaying respect. If you would like, fill in the name of a person you personally know (initials are fine) on the right side of the statement who practices that action. Then expand on the list with your ideas of why you respect people.

"We respect people who _____."

    ____ compliment us   ____ show us respect
    ____ display an interest in us   ____ listen to us
    ____ spend quality time with us   ____ praise our perseverance
    ____ provide us comfort   ____ show us empathy
    ____ display compassion for us   ____ are always there for us
    ____ nourish our body   ____ nourish our mind
    ____ nourish our soul   ____ maintain our trust
    ____ show us how to improve   ____ help fulfill our dreams

___ hold our hand
___ kick our rear to get us in gear
___ not unfairly judge, just help
___ build on our strengths
___ help us improve
___ display appropriate affection
___ make us laugh
___ share their joys
___ encourage us
___ display kindness to us
___ protect us
___ share inspiration, not insults
___ challenge us
___ are happy to see us
___ treat others fairly
___ keep their word
___ display love to us
___ are genuine
___ discipline us fairly
___ support our goals
___ support our faith
___ see the best in us
___ help us bounce
___ appreciate our interests
___ praise our attempts
___ help preserve our passion
___ forgive our inequities
___ accept us as we are
___ respect themselves
___ appreciate our being
___ care about us
___ help us balance our pride and humility
___ consider our wishes
___ help, not hurt
___ seek our opinions
___ brag about themselves
___ state facts, not attacks
___ notice our needs
___ express sentiment
___ practice patience
___ help us plan
___ share their compassion
___ help us feel physically safe
___ overlook our imperfections
___ share their gifts
___ display pride in our culture
___ "_____"
___ "_____"
___ "_____"
___ "_____"

___ pat our back
___ understand our fears
___ accept us where we are
___ are role models for us
___ display cooperation
___ laugh with us
___ share their imaginations
___ share their time
___ congratulate us
___ suggest ideas
___ help us through dark times
___ teach us
___ display proper manners
___ offer condolences
___ help us organize
___ empower us
___ love us
___ say positive things
___ set parameters for us
___ help us dream
___ show us dignity
___ help us see the best in ourselves
___ help us celebrate
___ admire our progress
___ keep us going
___ appreciate our presence
___ accept our inconsistencies
___ love their life
___ acknowledge our accomplishments
___ have time for us
___ converse, not just compete
___ respect our welfare
___ listen to our wants
___ respect our opinions
___ avoid listening to us
___ explain, not argue
___ avoid dwelling on past mistakes
___ capture our curiosity
___ communicate clearly with compassion
___ make us smile
___ bring us joy
___ make us feel uncomfortable
___ help us feel emotionally secure
___ praise our talents
___ avoid living their life through us
___ we treasure as role models
___ "_____"
___ "_____"
___ "_____"
___ "_____"

• CHECK

"If you want to be respected, you must respect yourself" —Spanish Proverb

Let's check the mirror. Imagine several of your acquaintances got together and checked the preceding listing regarding their respect for you. Drum roll please…. You do it for them. Fill in the blanks below imagining what your acquaintances would say about how you display respect to them…gulp!

Use a plus (+) for what you do and a minus (−) for what you do not do.

"People respect me because I _____."

_____ compliment them
_____ display an interest in them
_____ listen to them
_____ offer them opportunities
_____ show them empathy
_____ am always there for them
_____ nourish their mind
_____ preserve their confidences
_____ help them fulfill their dreams
_____ pat their back
_____ understand their fears
_____ accept them where they are
_____ act as a role model for them
_____ laugh with them
_____ share their joys
_____ treat them fairly
_____ encourage them
_____ help them be organized
_____ help them improve
_____ display kindness to them
_____ protect them
_____ share inspiration, not insults
_____ unfairly criticize them
_____ am happy to see them
_____ keep my word
_____ display love to them
_____ display how genuine I am to them
_____ discipline them fairly
_____ support their goals
_____ support their faith
_____ see the best in them
_____ help them bounce
_____ encourage their wholesome interests
_____ praise their attempts
_____ help preserve their passion
_____ forgive their inequities
_____ accept them as the special gift they are
_____ help them respect themselves
_____ appreciate their being

_____ show them respect
_____ offer them attention
_____ spend time with them
_____ provide them comfort
_____ display compassion for them
_____ potentially nourish their body
_____ torment their soul
_____ show them how to improve
_____ hold their hand
_____ kick their rear to get them in gear
_____ don't unfairly judge, just help
_____ help them build on their strengths
_____ display appropriate affection to them
_____ make them laugh
_____ share my joys
_____ share quality time with them
_____ support them
_____ congratulate them
_____ display a cooperative attitude
_____ suggest ideas
_____ help them through dark times
_____ teach them
_____ display proper manners
_____ offer condolences
_____ empower them
_____ truly love them
_____ say positive things
_____ set parameters for them
_____ help them dream
_____ show them dignity
_____ help them see the best in me
_____ help them celebrate
_____ admire their progress
_____ help them keep going
_____ display appreciation for their presence
_____ accept their inconsistencies
_____ help them love their life
_____ acknowledge their accomplishments
_____ inquire about their needs

___ display how much I care about them

___ help them balance pride and humility

___ consider their wishes

___ help, not hurt

___ seek their opinions

___ ask them questions

___ listen to their facts, avoiding attacks

___ notice their needs

___ express my sentiment

___ practice patience

___ help them feel physically safe

___ overlook their imperfections

___ share my gifts

___ display pride in their culture

___ converse, not just compete

___ enhance their welfare

___ listen to their wants

___ respect their opinions

___ brag to them to show I'm better

___ listen to them explain, avoid arguing

___ avoid dwelling on their past mistakes

___ capture their curiosity

___ allow them to communicate

___ make them smile

___ help them feel emotionally secure

___ praise their talents

___ avoid living my life through them

___ treasure them as a special gift

___ " _____ "

___ " _____ "

___ " _____ "

___ " _____ "

___ " _____ "

___ " _____ "

___ " _____ "

___ " _____ "

___ " _____ "

___ " _____ "

___ " _____ "

___ " _____ "

___ " _____ "

___ " _____ "

___ " _____ "

___ " _____ "

➤ Place a plus (+) by the statements you would like to hear and say more often and a minus (−) by the statements you would like to hear and say less often.

**The Journey
from
Me to We**

___ "Me!"

___ "I want!"

___ "You are wrong!"

___ "Ha, ha, see, I told you so!"

___ "Why, oh why, do you even try?"

___ "Can't you ever do anything right?"

___ "I am really sorry, I was wrong."

___ "Can we start all over again?"

___ "I sure appreciate you!"

___ "What do you think?"

___ "Thank you!"

___ "We"

• CONFIDENCE

"A loving person lives in a loving world. A hostile person lives in a hostile world; everyone you meet is your mirror." —Ken Keyes, Jr.

➢ List and analyze one or two elements of respect on the following forms that you would like to improve in your life.

ASSESSING GOALS*

List your goal(s) and assign a number from 0 to 10 (10 being high) to each consideration of the goals setting process.

GOALS ➤➤➤➤➤➤➤➤➤ _____ _____
                                         (Primary Goal)   (Secondary Goal)

	Primary Goal	Secondary Goal
1. Level of need/passion	_____	_____
2. Level of desire to sacrifice	_____	_____
3. Level of research/planning	_____	_____
4. Level of action/skills	_____	_____
5. Ability to accept change	_____	_____
6. Ability to endure criticism	_____	_____
7. Available resources/assistance	_____	_____
8. Available time/energy	_____	_____
9. History of patience	_____	_____
10. History of commitment	_____	_____

Probability Index Total   _____   _____

Probability Index Scoring

90–100	. . . . . . Celebrate!	40–49	. . . . . . Should you reassess your goal?
80–89	. . . . Go for it!	30–39	. . . . . . Was your addition correct?
70–79	. . . . Have you analyzed obstacles?	20–29	. . . . . . Did you follow the directions?
60–69	. . . . Can you change anything?	10–19	. . . . . . Is it time for a reality check?
50–59	. . . . Is it worth the risk?	0–9	. . . . . . Possibly seek professional help?

*Greatness Only Awaits Labor…Staaaaaaaaaart!

_____

(CHAPTER TITLE)

_____

(GOAL/VISION/DREAM)

There is a need because:

_____

_____

The change, sacrifices and criticism that need to be addressed are:

_____

_____

_____

The assistance and resources that need to be procured are:

_____

_____

The history of patience and commitment has been:

_____

_____

In order to reach the goal I will:

_____

_____

_____

_____

_____

_____

_____

The beginning timeline is:

Set Goals	Planning	Implement	Completion?	Completed!
___/___/_____	___/___/_____	___/___/_____	___/___/_____	___/___/_____

The celebration plans are:

_____

_____

_____

(CHAPTER TITLE)

_____

(GOAL/VISION/DREAM)

There is a need because:

_____

_____

The change, sacrifices and criticism that need to be addressed are:

_____

_____

_____

The assistance and resources that need to be procured are:

_____

_____

The history of patience and commitment has been:

_____

_____

In order to reach the goal I will:

_____

_____

_____

_____

_____

_____

_____

The beginning timeline is:

Set Goals	Planning	Implement	Completion?	Completed!
___/___/_____	___/___/_____	___/___/_____	___/___/_____	___/___/_____

The celebration plans are:

_____

_____

Indicate the acronyms that will assist you in remembering the elements of respect.

DREAMS	Desire Reflects Eventual Achievements Magically Secured
EGOTIST	Everybody Gags On The Individual's Selfish Traits
HELP	Hurry, Everyone Loves Progress
KIND	Keep It Nice, Dear
KINDNESS	Keep Intentions Nice Deescalate Negative Events'n Situations Swiftly
MANNERS	Make All Notions Nice, Every Response Sincere
MESSAGE	Making Every Statement Significant Allowing Goodness to Enter
NICE	Never Insult; Compliment Everyone
NOW	Never Overlook Wishes
REALITY	Recognizing Eventualities, Accepting Life's Inequities Teaches You
REWARD	Realizing Everyone's Work Assures Recognition Deserved
SMILE	Sure Makes It Lots Easier
SUCCESS	Seek Understanding Carefully; Character Eventually Sows Satisfaction
TEAM	Tolerance Empowers All Members
THANKS	To Honestly Acknowledge Noble Kindness Shown

RESPECT

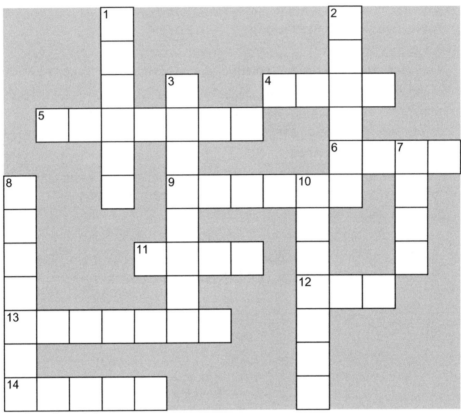

www.CharacterConstructionCompany.com

ACROSS

4 Tolerance Empowers All Members
5 Recognizing Eventualities, Accepting Life's Inequities Teaches You
6 Keep It Nice Dear
9 Desire Reflects Eventual Achievements Magically Secured
11 Hurry Everyone Loves Progress
12 Never Overlook Wishes
13 Everybody Gags On The Individual's Selfish Traits
14 Sure Makes It Lots Easier

DOWN

1 Realizing Everyone's Work Assures Recognition Deserved
2 To Honestly Acknowledge Noble Kindness Shown
3 Keep Intentions Nice De-escalate Events'n Situations Swiftly
7 Never Insult Compliment Everyone
8 Seek Understanding Carefully; Character Eventually Sows Satisfaction
10 Make All Notions Nice Every Response Sincere

RESPECT

Find the words in the grid. When you are done, the unused letters in the grid will spell out a hidden message. Pick them out from left to right, top line to bottom line. Words can go horizontally, vertically and diagonally in all eight directions.

```
N   E   K   W   V   E   R   M   Y   K
S   I   N   I   O   S   A   U   T   I
S   L   T   C   N   N   O   M   I   N
E   E   C   I   N   D   T   S   L   D
C   P   L   E   R   S   K   M   A   N
C   I   R   A   I   N   M   A   E   E
U   S   W   T   A   E   N   E   R   S
S   E   O   H   E   L   P   R   T   S
R   G   T   E   V   A   E   D   R   Y
E   O   N   E   L   S   M   I   L   E
```

DREAMS	NOW
EGOTIST	REALITY
HELP	REWARD
KIND	SMILE
KINDNESS	SUCCESS
MANNERS	TEAM
NICE	THANKS

ACHIEVEMENT
Always Cooperate, Honest Individuals Ensure
Victory Eventually; Make Every Notion True

• CONNECT

Discovering the steps required to achieve life's goals

Our _____ (**D**esire **R**eflects **E**ventual **A**chievements **M**agically **S**ecured)

and _____ (**V**ery **I**ntense **S**tatement **I**ndicating **O**bjectives **N**ecessary)

of _____ (**S**ecuring **E**steem **L**essens **F**ear; **W**orking **O**ffers **R**espect **T**riggering

Happiness) become _____ (**R**ealizing **E**vents, **A**ccepting **L**ife's **I**nequities **T**eaches

Individuals **E**verlasting **S**tructure) if we _____ (**L**ove **E**ducation, **A**chieve **R**espect **N**ow)

to develop our _____ (**T**o **A**chieve, **L**atent **E**nergy **N**eeds **T**raining) leading us to

_____ (**S**eek **U**nderstanding **C**arefully; **C**haracter **E**ventually **S**ows **S**atisfaction).

• CHALLENGE

Developing visions and establishing goals

1. Pursuing interests and strengths to fulfill your vision:

➤ Regardless of your current obligations and responsibilities—
    List your natural talents and interests.

_____   _____

_____   _____

➤ Regardless of your current obligations and responsibilities—
    List the ways you enjoy spending your leisure time.

_____   _____

_____   _____

2. Accepting an identity based on accomplishments:

➢ What would your acquaintances list as your accomplishments?

_____

_____

_____

_____

3. Developing a desire to be competitive:

➢ What types of competitions do you enjoy participating in?

_____

_____

_____

_____

4. Avoiding mediocrity:

➢ What activities have you attempted that ended in failure?

_____

_____

_____

_____

5. Discovering role models:

➢ List the people who have become your role models because they followed their passion to develop their talents while pursuing their visions.

_____

_____

_____

_____

6. Establishing goals:

➤ What is a goal that one of your role models attained?

_____

7. Establishing a plan of action:

➤ What actions did your role model pursue to attain their goal?

_____

_____

_____

8. Learning to endure criticism:

➤ List several negative statements that have been made about your role model.

_____

_____

_____

_____

9. Celebrating accomplishments:

➤ What benefits has your role model received to help them celebrate reaching their goal?

_____

_____

_____

_____

• CHANNEL

Clarify the steps in achieving the goals you envision

1. Pursuing interests and talents:

➤ Regardless of your current obligations and responsibilities, what would you like to be involved in to enable you to combine your interests and talents?

_____

_____

_____

_____

_____

2. Accepting an identity based on accomplishments:

➤ What do you DESIRE (**D**oes **E**veryone **S**trive **I**n **R**eaching **E**xcellence) to be known for accomplishing?

_____

_____

_____

_____

_____

3. Developing a desire to be competitive:

➤ If you could start all over again, what activities would you like to be able to compete in?

_____

_____

_____

_____

_____

4. Avoiding mediocrity:

➤ What aspects of your existence seem to be on the fringe of MEDIOCRITY?
(**M**uddle through **E**very **D**ay **I**nsisting **O**n **C**rummy **R**esults **I**nfamously **T**opnotch to **Y**ou).

_____

_____

_____

_____

5. Discovering role models:

➤ Who are your role models in several aspects of your life?

ASPECTS	PEOPLE
_____	_____
_____	_____
_____	_____
_____	_____

6. Establishing a set of goals:

➤ Considering your passions, interests, talents, and role models, what do you HOPE
(**H**arnessing **O**ptimism **P**roduces **E**mpowerment) to achieve? (This might even become
a totally new direction for your life)

_____

_____

_____

_____

7. Establishing a plan of action:

➤ What do you need to start doing to realize those accomplishments?

_____

_____

_____

8. Learning to endure criticism:

➢ What negative statements will others make regarding your pursuits?

_____

_____

_____

_____

9. Celebrating accomplishments:

➢ How will you determine if you have attained your desired level of success?

_____

_____

_____

➢ How will you celebrate that success?

_____

_____

_____

• CHECK

"Opportunity is missed by most because it is dressed in overalls and looks like work."
—Thomas Edison

• CONFIDENCE

"It is never too late to be what you might have been." —George Eliot

➢ Hopefully, you have realized what brings fulfillment to your life. This process may have shined the light on a need for change to achieve success. Please list one or two goals on the following forms to determine if you are on the path to achieving the success that you desire or if you would like to change your direction!

ASSESSING GOALS*

*List your goal(s) and assign a number from 0 to 10 (10 being high)
to each consideration of the goals setting process.*

GOALS ▸▸▸▸▸▸▸▸▸ _____   _____
(Primary Goal)   (Secondary Goal)

	Primary Goal	Secondary Goal
1. Level of need/passion	_____	_____
2. Level of desire to sacrifice	_____	_____
3. Level of research/planning	_____	_____
4. Level of action/skills	_____	_____
5. Ability to accept change	_____	_____
6. Ability to endure criticism	_____	_____
7. Available resources/assistance	_____	_____
8. Available time/energy	_____	_____
9. History of patience	_____	_____
10. History of commitment	_____	_____

Probability Index Total   _____   _____

Probability Index Scoring

90–100 . . . . . . Celebrate!		40–49 . . . . . . Should you reassess your goal?
80–89 . . . . Go for it!		30–39 . . . . . . Was your addition correct?
70–79 . . . . Have you analyzed obstacles?		20–29 . . . . . . Did you follow the directions?
60–69 . . . . Can you change anything?		10–19 . . . . . . Is it time for a reality check?
50–59 . . . . Is it worth the risk?		0–9 . . . . . . Possibly seek professional help?

*Greatness Only Awaits Labor…Staaaaaaaaart!

_____

(CHAPTER TITLE)

_____

(GOAL/VISION/DREAM)

There is a need because:

_____

_____

The change, sacrifices and criticism that need to be addressed are:

_____

_____

_____

The assistance and resources that need to be procured are:

_____

_____

The history of patience and commitment has been:

_____

_____

In order to reach the goal I will:

_____

_____

_____

_____

_____

_____

_____

The beginning timeline is:

Set Goals	Planning	Implement	Completion?	Completed!
___/___/_____	___/___/_____	___/___/_____	___/___/_____	___/___/_____

The celebration plans are:

_____

_____

_____

(CHAPTER TITLE)

_____

(GOAL/VISION/DREAM)

There is a need because:

_____

_____

The change, sacrifices and criticism that need to be addressed are:

_____

_____

_____

The assistance and resources that need to be procured are:

_____

_____

The history of patience and commitment has been:

_____

_____

In order to reach the goal I will:

_____

_____

_____

_____

_____

_____

_____

The beginning timeline is:

Set Goals	Planning	Implement	Completion?	Completed!
___/___/____	___/___/____	___/___/____	___/___/____	___/___/____

The celebration plans are:

_____

_____

Indicate the acronyms that will help you achieve your goals.

APATHY	Awaiting People's Actions To Help You
BOSS	Big On Securing Success
CAN DO	Control All Negativism; Develop Optimism
ENJOY	Everyone Now Journey Over Yonder
DREAMS	Desire Reflects Eventual Achievements Magically Secured
GOALS	Greatness Only Awaits Labor—Staaaaaart
HOPE	Harnessing Optimism Produces Empowerment
IMPROVE	Individuals Make Progress Rewarding Our Valiant Efforts
JOYFUL	Journey Over Yonder, Forget Unnecessary Lumps
LAZY	Losers Always Zap Ya
LEARN	Love Education, Achieve Respect Now
MEDIOCRITY	Muddle through Every Day Insisting On Crummy Results Infamously Topnotch to You
MODEL	Making Observations Determines Every Liking
PLAN	Please Learn All Necessities
PROGRESS	People Reform Or Garner Refinement Establishing Some Success
QUITTER	Quick, Understand: Initiative Takes Thorough Extensive Repetition
REALITIES	Realizing Events Accepting Life's Inequities Teaches Individuals Everlasting Structure
RISK	Resourceful Individuals Secure Karma
SELF-WORTH	Securing Esteem Lessens Fear; Working Offers Respect, Triggering Happiness
TALENT	To Achieve, Latent Energy Needs Training
VISION	Very Intense Statement Indicating Objectives Necessary
WIMP	Woe Is Me Person
WORK HARD	We Only Respect Kindness; Happiness Always Rewards Dedication

ACHIEVEMENT

www.CharacterConstructionCompany.com

ACROSS

1 Woe Is Me Person
4 Harnessing Optimism Produces Empowerment
6 Love Education Achieve Respect Now
8 Greatness Only Awaits Labor Start
10 Securing Esteem Lessens Fear Working Offers Respect Triggering Happiness
12 Everybody Now Journey Over Yonder
14 Desire Reflects Eventual Achievements Magically Secured
16 Making Observations Determines Every Liking
18 Losers Always Zap Ya
19 Quick Understand Initiative Takes Thorough Extensive Repetition
22 Very Intense Statement Indicating Objectives Necessary
23 People Reform Or Garner Refinement Establishing Some Success

DOWN

2 Please Learn All Necessities
3 We Only Respect Kindness; Happiness Always Rewards Dedication
5 Realizing Events Accepting Life's Inequities Teaches Individuals Everlasting Structure
7 Journey Over Yonder Forget Unnecessary Lumps
9 Muddle through Everyday Insisting On Crummy Results Infamously Topnotch to You
11 Awaiting People's Actions To Help You
13 To Achieve Latent Energy Needs Training
15 Individuals Make Progress Rewarding Our Valiant Efforts
17 Control All Negativism Develop Optimism
20 Big On Securing Success
21 Resourceful Individuals Secure Karma

ACHIEVEMENT

Find the words in the grid. When you are done, the unused letters in the grid will spell out a hidden message. Pick them out from left to right, top line to bottom line. Words can go horizontally, vertically and diagonally in all eight directions.

```
W  O  R  K  H  A  R  D  D  S  S  E  S  I
R  E  R  E  F  L  N  E  M  S  S  H  C  Y
T  T  Y  S  S  R  E  A  O  E  V  O  E  T
N  N  T  H  A  E  E  B  I  U  Q  P  A  I
L  E  P  E  T  R  L  T  W  U  A  E  R  R
C  L  L  E  D  A  I  F  I  I  H  I  I  C
L  A  A  E  N  L  P  T  W  V  M  V  S  O
U  T  N  E  A  J  T  A  I  O  M  P  K  I
F  E  L  E  N  E  O  S  T  S  R  M  A  D
Y  G  R  E  R  I  I  Y  C  A  L  T  Y  E
O  S  E  C  D  O  C  A  N  D  O  U  H  M
J  R  E  D  N  O  P  R  O  G  R  E  S  S
X  G  H  N  B  B  M  E  V  O  R  P  M  I
B  S  L  A  O  G  M  R  J  Y  Z  A  L  K
```

APATHY	JOYFUL	REALITIES
BOSS	LAZY	RISK
CANDO	LEARN	SELFWORTH
DREAMS	MEDIOCRITY	TALENT
ENJOY	MODEL	VISION
GOALS	PLAN	WIMP
HOPE	PROGRESS	WORKHARD
IMPROVE	QUITTER	

CHOICES
Citizens Have Opportunities In
Commitment'n Every Situation

- ## CONNECT
  Every human action involves a decision

  We should avoid _____ (All Beings Underestimate Some Eventualities) by

  allowing our _____ (Categorizing Our Notions, Selecting Choices, Influences

  Everyone's Noticeable Character Eventually) to interpret _____ (Every Vicious

  Individual Loses), _____ (Regulating Us Leads Everyone Successfully),

  and _____ (Learn Allowable Ways). Then we can make use of our

  _____ (Walking In The Spirit) so our _____ (Walking

  In Spirit Directing Our Memories) prevails and we _____ (Walk Our Words)

  everyone.

- ## CHALLENGE
  Deciding what helps and what hurts

  1. Avoiding situations or substances that interfere with peace of mind:

  ➤ List situations and substances that your friends, family, and associates should avoid to help them
     maintain their peace of mind.

SITUATIONS	SUBSTANCES
_____	_____
_____	_____
_____	_____
_____	_____

2. Learning the steps in making decisions:

➤ Place a check on the following points that should be considered while making decisions.

    ____ Does it seem logical and reasonable?

    ____ Would it be alright if everyone did this?

    ____ How will your actions affect you and others?

    ____ Will you think well of yourself when you look back on it?

    ____ How would the person you admire the most handle this?

    ____ Would you want your family and friends to know?

3. Determining right from wrong:

➤ Fill in one word that helps you determine what is right and what is wrong.

"I know it is usually wrong if it _____ someone."

"I know it is usually right if it _____ someone."

4. Avoiding being hypocritical:

➤ Fill in one eight-letter word that can be the trigger for hypocrisy.

"Explaining what we plan to do can easily evolve into making

a _____ which may not come true."

5. Learning to walk our words:

➤ Fill in the acronym for walking our words.

"If we simply walk our words we can _____ others with our actions."

6. Steps in filtering what enters our minds and bodies:

➤ Fill in the missing words.

"We have a choice of:

Goodness in and _____ out or garbage in and _____ out."

- **CHANNEL**

  Let's analyze some of your current choices.

  1. Avoiding situations or substances that interfere with peace of mind:

  ➤ Explain how you have helped an acquaintance avoid a situation
     or substance that would have interfered with their peace of mind.

  _____

  _____

  _____

  _____

  2. Learning the steps in making decisions:

  ➤ Explain how an acquaintance of yours made a decision based on the
     wrong reasons that resulted in causing problems.

  _____

  _____

  _____

  _____

  3. Determining right from wrong:

  ➤ Explain how you made a decision to go forward with a situation
     even though others told you it was wrong.

  _____

  _____

  _____

  _____

4. Avoiding being hypocritical:

➢ Describe a situation when someone promised you
something but did not make good on that promise.

_____

_____

_____

_____

5. Learning to walk our words:

➢ List some of your recent accomplishments that you
did not tell anyone you were going to try; you just did them.

_____

_____

_____

_____

6. Filtering what enters our minds and bodies:

➢ What situations and substances do you block from entering your mind and body?

SITUATIONS   **SUBSTANCES**

_____   _____

_____   _____

_____   _____

_____   _____

- ## CHECK

  "It is our choices that show what we really are,
  far more than our abilities." —J. K. Rowling

- ## CONFIDENCE

  "Life is a sum of all of your choices." —Voltaire

  ➤ List one, possibly two of your goals involving your choices on the following forms.

ASSESSING GOALS*

*List your goal(s) and assign a number from 0 to 10 (10 being high)
to each consideration of the goals setting process.*

GOALS ➤➤➤➤➤➤➤➤➤ _____   _____

                                                    (Primary Goal)   (Secondary Goal)

	Primary Goal	Secondary Goal
1. Level of need/passion	____	____
2. Level of desire to sacrifice	____	____
3. Level of research/planning	____	____
4. Level of action/skills	____	____
5. Ability to accept change	____	____
6. Ability to endure criticism	____	____
7. Available resources/assistance	____	____
8. Available time/energy	____	____
9. History of patience	____	____
10. History of commitment	____	____

Probability Index Total   ____   ____

Probability Index Scoring

90–100 . . . . . . Celebrate!	40–49 . . . . . . Should you reassess your goal?
80–89 . . . . Go for it!	30–39 . . . . . . Was your addition correct?
70–79 . . . . Have you analyzed obstacles?	20–29 . . . . . . Did you follow the directions?
60–69 . . . . Can you change anything?	10–19 . . . . . . Is it time for a reality check?
50–59 . . . . Is it worth the risk?	0–9 . . . . . . Possibly seek professional help?

*Greatness Only Awaits Labor…Staaaaaaaaaart!

_____

(CHAPTER TITLE)

_____

(GOAL/VISION/DREAM)

There is a need because:

_____

_____

The change, sacrifices and criticism that need to be addressed are:

_____

_____

_____

The assistance and resources that need to be procured are:

_____

_____

The history of patience and commitment has been:

_____

_____

In order to reach the goal I will:

_____

_____

_____

_____

_____

_____

The beginning timeline is:

Set Goals	Planning	Implement	Completion?	Completed!
___/___/_____	___/___/_____	___/___/_____	___/___/_____	___/___/_____

The celebration plans are:

_____

_____

_____

(CHAPTER TITLE)

_____

(GOAL/VISION/DREAM)

There is a need because:

_____

_____

The change, sacrifices and criticism that need to be addressed are:

_____

_____

_____

The assistance and resources that need to be procured are:

_____

_____

The history of patience and commitment has been:

_____

_____

In order to reach the goal I will:

_____

_____

_____

_____

_____

_____

_____

The beginning timeline is:

Set Goals	Planning	Implement	Completion?	Completed!
___/___/_____	___/___/_____	___/___/_____	___/___/_____	___/___/_____

The celebration plans are:

_____

_____

Indicate the acronyms that will help you achieve your goals.

ABUSE	All Beings Underestimate Some Eventualities
ALCOHOL	Always Limit Consumption, Often Hinders Our Lives
ARREST	A Required Reservation Employing Self-discipline Training
CARE	Courage Always Resonates Endearingly
CONSCIENCE	Categorizing Our Notions, Selecting Choices, Influences Everyone's Noticeable Character Eventually
EVIL	Every Vicious Individual Loses
FREEDOM	Forget Restrictions, Enjoy Every Day's Opportunistic Moments
LAW	Learn Allowable Ways
LOVE	Lights On, Very Empowering
MUSIC	Mankind's Ultimate Study In Creation
PASSION	People Always Seek Success If Opportunity's Noble
POLICE	Politeness Only Lasts If Citizens Empathize
REALITY	Recognizing Eventualities, Accepting Life's Inequities Teaches You
RULES	Regulating Us Leads Everyone to Success
TIME	Teaming Insures More Efficiency
US	Understand Self
WANT	Wishes Always Need Time
WHAT IF	We're Happiest Always Thinking, Initiating Fantasies
WISDOM	Walk In Spirit Directing Our Memories
WITS	Walk In The Spirit
WOW	Walk Our Words

CHOICES

www.CharacterConstructionCompany.com

ACROSS

2 Walk Our Words

6 Learn Allowable Ways

9 Walking In Spirit Directing Our Memories

10 A Required Reservation Employing Self-discipline Training

12 Teaming Insures More Efficiency

13 Lights On Very Empowering

14 Understand Self

15 Every Vicious Individual Loses

16 People Always Seek Success If Opportunity's Noble

18 Recognizing Eventualities Accepting Life's Inequities Teaches You

19 Mankind's Ultimate Study In Creation

20 Forget Restrictions Enjoy Every Delightful Opportunistic Moment

DOWN

1 Categorizing Our Notions Selecting Choices Influences Everyone's Noticeable Character Eventually

3 Wishes Always Need Time

4 Always Limit Consumption Often Hinders Our Lives

5 Politeness Only Lasts If Citizens Empathize

7 We're Happiest Always Thinking Initiating Fantasies

8 Courage Always Resonates Endearingly

9 Walk In The Spirit

11 Regulating Us Leads Everyone to Success

17 All Beings Underestimate Some Eventualities

CHOICES

Find the words in the grid. When you are done, the unused letters in the grid will spell out a hidden message. Pick them out from left to right, top line to bottom line. Words can go horizontally, vertically and diagonally in all eight directions.

```
W  C  A  M  O  D  E  E  R  F  L  L
T  O  E  P  A  S  S  I  O  N  O  R
N  N  V  A  R  R  E  S  T  H  K  E
A  S  O  I  E  N  T  H  O  E  S  A
W  C  L  F  S  P  P  C  I  R  I  L
T  I  N  I  U  T  L  O  R  N  E  I
W  E  X  T  B  A  I  U  L  V  M  T
I  N  R  A  A  C  L  W  I  I  C  Y
S  C  L  H  W  E  A  L  T  I  C  L
D  E  W  W  S  A  F  R  S  D  W  E
O  V  E  M  I  T  L  U  E  O  S  L
M  Z  L  Z  T  V  M  K  W  V  R  U
```

www.CharacterConstructionCompany.com

ABUSE	LAW	TIME
ALCOHOL	LOVE	US
ARREST	MUSIC	WANT
CARE	PASSION	WHATIF
CONSCIENCE	POLICE	WISDOM
EVIL	REALITY	WITS
FREEDOM	RULES	WOW

TRUST
To Rely Upon Someone's Tenacity

- ## CONNECT
  To develop faith in our actions and the actions of others

  We all _____ (**H**arnessing **O**ptimism **P**roduces **E**mpowerment) the _____

  (**P**oliteness **O**nly **L**asts **I**f **C**itizens **E**mpathize) will _____ (**H**urry, **E**verybody **L**oves

  Progress) if a _____ (**S**ure, **E**veryone **L**oves **F**ulfilling **I**ndividual **S**uccess'n

  Happiness) person adds _____ (**S**ome **T**hink **R**ealistic **E**ffort **S**aves **S**anity) to our

  life by attempting to _____ (**S**ometimes **T**rusting **E**veryone **A**ctivates **L**oss) from us.

- ## CHALLENGE
  To be able to accomplish stressful tasks

  1. Envisioning situations in advance:

  ➤ Give an example of a stressful situation where you were successful because you envisioned the situation in advance.

  _____

  _____

  _____

  _____

  _____

  2. Taking the initiative to help:

  ➤ Describe an incident similar to the above where you refused to help because of the risks involved.

  _____

  _____

  _____

  _____

  _____

3. Quantifying the risks involved:

➤ List several of the risks involved in the situation you described.

_____

_____

_____

_____

4. Analyzing who can be relied upon:

➤ Provide the names, or initials, of who would have helped.

_____

5. Recognizing who needs to be the most reliable:

➤ Do you wish that you would have helped?

Yes _____

No _____

• CHANNEL

"Spread love wherever you go. Let no one ever come to you without leaving happier." —Mother Teresa

1. Envisioning situations to display trust:

➤ Draw a plus sign (+) next to the words that build trustworthiness.
   Draw a minus sign (−) by the words that potentially diminish trust.

__acceptance	__hate	__promise	__designate	__understanding
__comfort	__rejection	__confidence	__truthful	__self-centered
__forgiving	__rob	__abandonment	__secretive	__whisper
__fear	__hide	__betray	__sincere	__late
__inconsistent	__failure	__lie	__mistake	__gossip
__bluff	__steal	__exaggerate	__inconsiderate	__caring
__exonerate	__kind	__deceive	__reliable	__authentic
__faithful	__believe	__safe	__loving	__truthful
__perfect	__sincere	__rumor	__golden rule	__dishonest
__sharing	__loyal	__compassionate	__thoughtful	__honest

__integrity   __respect   __inspirational   __disrespect   __judgmental

__critical   __sarcasm   __egotist   __fabrication   __organized

(Add additional words similar to the above list)

TRUSTWORTHINESS	LACK OF TRUST
_____	_____
_____	_____
_____	_____
_____	_____
_____	_____

2. Taking the initiative to help:

➤ Explain how you felt after you failed to help someone.

_____

_____

_____

_____

_____

3. Quantifying the risks involved:

➤ What is absolutely the worst thing that could have happened if you would have helped?

_____

_____

_____

_____

_____

4. Analyzing the people you feel you can rely upon:

➤ Who can you rely upon and why?

PERSON   **WHY**

_____   _____

_____   _____

_____   _____

_____   _____

_____   _____

5. Recognizing who needs to be the most trustworthy:

➤ Check the most appropriate answer.

_____ A stranger

_____ A friend

_____ A family member

_____ Myself

• CHECK

"Life is a shipwreck but we must not forget to sing in the life boats." —Voltaire

• CONFIDENCE

"The weak can never forgive. Forgiveness is the attribute of the strong." —Gandhi

A lifetime of trust can be obliterated by one inappropriate statement or an inappropriate action. We should ACT (**A**lways **C**arefully **T**read) accordingly to hopefully maintain the trust of others. If trust is breached, imparting forgiveness empowers us to begin the process of rebuilding trust. List one or two names on the goals forms of individuals you would like to forgive (initials are fine).

ASSESSING GOALS*

List your goal(s) and assign a number from 0 to 10 (10 being high) to each consideration of the goals setting process.

GOALS ▸▸▸▸▸▸▸▸▸ _____ _____
                          (Primary Goal)   (Secondary Goal)

1. Level of need/passion   _____   _____
2. Level of desire to sacrifice   _____   _____
3. Level of research/planning   _____   _____
4. Level of action/skills   _____   _____
5. Ability to accept change   _____   _____
6. Ability to endure criticism   _____   _____
7. Available resources/assistance   _____   _____
8. Available time/energy   _____   _____
9. History of patience   _____   _____
10. History of commitment   _____   _____

Probability Index Total   _____   _____

Probability Index Scoring

90–100 . . . . . . Celebrate!   40–49 . . . . . . Should you reassess your goal?
80–89 . . . . Go for it!   30–39 . . . . . . Was your addition correct?
70–79 . . . . Have you analyzed obstacles? 20–29 . . . . . . Did you follow the directions?
60–69 . . . . Can you change anything?   10–19 . . . . . . Is it time for a reality check?
50–59 . . . . Is it worth the risk?   0–9 . . . . . . Possibly seek professional help?

*Greatness Only Awaits Labor…Staaaaaaaaaart!

_____

(CHAPTER TITLE)

_____

(GOAL/VISION/DREAM)

There is a need because:

_____

_____

The change, sacrifices and criticism that need to be addressed are:

_____

_____

_____

The assistance and resources that need to be procured are:

_____

_____

The history of patience and commitment has been:

_____

_____

In order to reach the goal I will:

_____

_____

_____

_____

_____

_____

_____

The beginning timeline is:

Set Goals	Planning	Implement	Completion?	Completed!
___/___/____	___/___/____	___/___/____	___/___/____	___/___/____

The celebration plans are:

_____

_____

_____

(CHAPTER TITLE)

_____

(GOAL/VISION/DREAM)

There is a need because:

_____

_____

The change, sacrifices and criticism that need to be addressed are:

_____

_____

_____

The assistance and resources that need to be procured are:

_____

_____

The history of patience and commitment has been:

_____

_____

In order to reach the goal I will:

_____

_____

_____

_____

_____

_____

_____

The beginning timeline is:

Set Goals	Planning	Implement	Completion?	Completed!
___/___/____	___/___/____	___/___/____	___/___/____	___/___/____

The celebration plans are:

_____

_____

Indicate the acronyms that will help you achieve your goals.

CHOIR	Caring Hearts Offer Inspired Relationships
FEEL	Faith Eventually Elevates Love
HEALTH	Hopefully Everyone Accesses Life's Trip Happily
HELP	Hurry, Everyone Loves Progress
HOPE	Harnessing Optimism Produces Empowerment
MUSIC	Mankind's Ultimate Study In Creation
PLAN	Please Learn All Necessities
POLICE	Politeness Only Lasts If Citizens Empathize
RISK	Resourceful Individuals Secure Karma
SELFISH	Sure, Everyone Loves Fulfilling Individual Success'n Happiness
STEAL	Sometimes Trusting Everyone Activates Loss
STRESS	Some Think Realistic Effort Saves Sanity

TRUST

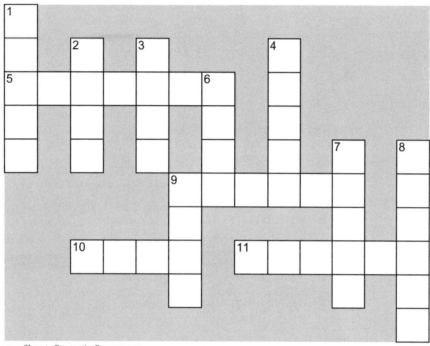

www.CharacterConstructionCompany.com

ACROSS

5 Sure Everyone Loves Fulfilling Individual Success'n Happiness

9 Hopefully Everyone Accesses Life's Trip Happily

10 Faith Eventually Elevates Love

11 Politeness Only Lasts If Citizens Empathize

DOWN

1 Mankind's Ultimate Study In Creation

2 Please Learn All Necessities

3 Resourceful Individuals Secure Karma

4 Sometimes Trusting Everyone Activates Loss

6 Harnessing Optimism Produces Empowerment

7 Caring Hearts Offer Inspired Relationships

8 Some Think Realistic Effort Saves Sanity

9 Hurry Everyone Loves Progress

TRUST

Find the words in the grid. When you are done, the unused letters in the grid will spell out a hidden message. Pick them out from left to right, top line to bottom line. Words can go horizontally, vertically and diagonally in all eight directions.

```
L  R  S  O  C  M  K  Y  O  U
R  I  D  T  U  O  N  A  L  P
O  O  S  S  R  R  S  P  H  J
D  H  I  E  E  E  W  D  O  D
W  C  L  L  L  C  S  Y  P  K
N  H  E  A  K  F  I  S  E  S
X  E  E  B  T  Q  I  L  M  I
F  T  R  L  L  R  P  S  O  R
S  L  G  Q  P  Y  N  L  H  P
H  E  A  L  T  H  Q  R  M  B
```

CHOIR	PLAN
FEEL	POLICE
HEALTH	RISK
HELP	SELFISH
HOPE	STEAL
MUSIC	STRESS

EMPOWERMENT
Everyone Manages Productive Opportunities With Each Response, Mending Every Negative Thought

- ## CONNECT
  Fulfilling needs from the other person's perspective

  _____ (**S**incere **A**ttitudes **L**aunch **E**veryone **S**uccessfully) is teaching and teaching is sales; it can simply _____ (**E**veryone **M**akes **P**ertinent **O**bservations **W**ith **E**very **R**esponse) people with _____ (**C**hanging **O**ur **N**egative **F**ears **I**nvites **D**elightful **E**xperiences, **N**ever **C**onsidered **E**asy) to _____ (**P**lease **L**earn **A**ll **N**ecessities) to reach their _____ (**G**reatness **O**nly **A**waits **L**abor…**S**tart). The _____ (**A**lways **R**espect **T**ruth) of always securing _____ (**P**roviding **R**evenue **O**pportunities **F**ulfills **I**ndividual **T**asks **S**uccessfully) in sales is not always _____ (**E**verybody **A**lways **S**ays **Y**es). If everyone was _____ (**G**olden **R**ule **E**levates **A**ll **T**eams) at it, most salespeople would be _____ (**B**ountiful **R**esources **O**nly **K**eep **E**scaping) and be out of a _____ (**J**ust **O**ver **B**roke).

- ## CHALLENGE
  Delegating your knowledge and power

  1. Developing listening skills:

  ➤ A vital component of effective listening skills is asking the appropriate questions to facilitate a meaningful discussion. Skillful questioning can lead to thought-provoking discussions and worthwhile information. The examples below list negative statements and positive statements side by side. Place a plus (+) next to the actions displaying good listening skills. Place a minus (−) next to the actions displaying inappropriate listening skills.

___Look the person straight in the eye	___Keep glancing around searching for friends
___Try to position yourself higher than speaker	___Assume a posture comforting for the speaker
___Turn to someone else and start talking	___Make eye contact with others to involve them
___Be in charge; try to control the conversation	___Breathe through your nose
___Answer your phone and begin talking	___Check your phone, potentially turn it off
___Look interested, smile, and add an occasional response	___Talk on your phone
___Disagree in the middle of the person's sentence	___Ask questions at appropriate times

___Listen twice as much as you talk

___Potentially take notes while listening

___Suggest a word they might be searching for

___Ask questions about the person's topic

___Tell the person you're tired of hearing about it

___Link it to your experiences to help remember it

___Attempt to pry confidential information

___If necessary, tell the person how much time you have

___If they are rude be KWIK (**K**ill **W**ith **I**nstant **K**indness)

___Potentially ask what you specifically need to know

___Interrupt so you won't forget what to say

___Show all of your feelings with facial expressions

___Imagine you'll be asked to repeat what was just said

___Display your impatience

___When you have the chance, talk only about yourself

___Check your messages

___Tell the person they aren't explaining it properly

___Avoid looking at the speaker

___Divulge confidential information to the person

___Say, "Don't you understand that?"

___Say, "I'll try to explain it a different way."

___Always try to tell a more impressive story

___Try to end every sentence for the person

___Amuse yourself with an electronic device

___If possible, change the subject

___Wait in silence, avoid all questions

___Say, "You've already convinced me of that."

___Isolate the information to avoid confusion

___Avoid asking inappropriate questions

___Ask, "Are you talking to me?"

___Talk twice as much as you listen

___Check your messages and/or read

___Say, "May I interject..."

___Display appropriate facial expressions

___Make a phone call

___Thank others, even if you aren't in agreement

___Keep asking questions about the person

___Potentially deactivate your electronics

___Possibly encourage the person to elaborate

___Notice eyes, inflections, expressions, etc.

___Acknowledge requests for confidentiality

___Say, "I'll try to explain it better."

___Say, "I've told you a thousand times that"

___Avoid trying to always have the best tale

(Add several more)

_____

_____

_____

_____

_____

_____

_____

_____

2. Becoming a catalyst:

➤ Check the following words that best describe serving as an effective catalyst.

_____Demanding

_____Asking

_____Criticizing

_____Helping

_____Delegating

_____Expediting

_____Telling

_____Complimenting

_____Facilitating

_____Ordering

_____Explaining

_____Teaching

3. Learning to receive and share life's joys:

➤ Place these words in the appropriate spaces—Love, Soul, Spirit.

JOYS: "**J**ust **O**pen **Y**our _____."

SOUL: "**S**ource **O**f **U**nconditional _____."

JOYS: "**J**ust **O**ffer **Y**our _____."

➤ Check and list the things that bring joy to your life.

____Favorite place to view a sunrise _____

____Freshly fallen snow in the _____

____Hearing raindrops hit the _____

____The aroma of _____

____The taste of_____

85

____The sight of _____

____A picture of _____

____Participating in team sports; name the sports _____

____Participating in individual sports; name them _____

____Participating in making music with a _____

____Shopping at _____

____Being with family for _____

____Being involved with community groups at _____

____Helping other people with _____

____My perfect job would be _____

____Being proud of _____

____Listening to music about _____

____Watching movies about _____

____Reading about _____

____Laughing with _____

____Displaying affection to _____

____Receiving affection from _____

____Receiving compliments from _____

____Giving compliments to _____

____Giving a hug to _____

____Receiving a hug from _____

____Riding in a _____

____Being at _____

____Visiting with _____

____Thinking about _____

____Being involved with _____

____Attending a ceremony at _____

____Forgiving others for _____

____Hoping to be forgiven for _____

____Spending time by _____

____The clock speeds up when I _____

____The clock slows down when I _____

____Fulfilling the challenge of _____

____Proving I excel at _____

____Working hard to _____

____Learning about _____

____Feeling more worthy because _____

____Telling the truth about _____

____Disregarding the drama created in my life about _____

____Establishing a better work ethic by _____

____Improving my reputation regarding _____

____Traveling to _____

____My most prized possessions are _____

____Favorite pets _____

____Watching the _____

____Listening to _____

____Developing more pride in _____

____Favorite place to view a sunset _____

____Hopes of _____

____Hopes of _____

___Hopes of _____

___Hopes of _____

___Hopes of _____

___Hopes of _____

___Memories of _____

___Memories of _____

___Memories of _____

___Memories of _____

___Memories of _____

___Memories of _____

(Add several more)

___ "_____" _____

___ "_____" _____

___ "_____" _____

___ "_____" _____

___ "_____" _____

➤ Circle one appropriate underlined word in each quote from the ABC book.

"We get what we <u>seek</u>   <u>want</u>   <u>give</u>   <u>demand</u>."

"We reap what we <u>want</u>   <u>get</u>   <u>sow</u>   <u>wish</u>."

"We are the person in the <u>center</u>   <u>mirror</u>   <u>middle</u>   <u>know</u>."

4. Approaching sales from the wants and needs of others:

➤ Check the most appropriate words for this approach.

_____Inquire

_____Ask

_____Inform

_____Force

_____Demand

_____Question

_____Listen

_____Pressure

_____Offer

_____Suggest

_____Coerce

_____Intimidate

5. Understanding the Seven Cs of Sales:

➤ Provide the numbers to align the "Seven Cs of Sales" in the proper order. You may wish to revisit this exercise.

_____Channel

_____Connect

_____Celebrate

_____Confidence

_____Courage

_____Check

_____Challenge

6. Comprehending that sales is teaching and teaching is sales:

➤ Sales is teaching and teaching is sales. It involves empowering others with the knowledge of the (circle the most important word) price   value   uniqueness   availability of an idea, product, or service.

• CHANNEL

Don't just listen to what I say. Listen to what I mean.

1. Developing listening skills:

➤ Active listening is the key to paying attention and learning from others. What might help you become a more effective active listener?

_____

_____

_____

_____

2. Serving as a catalyst:

➤ Delegating responsibilities is a very effective method of becoming a catalyst. What tasks can you ask others to assist you with to help decrease the stress in your life and potentially lead others to more success?

TASKS	PERSON

3. Learning to receive and share life's joys:

➤ List the wholesome joys you would like to receive more of in your life and who you would like to share those joys with.

JOYS	PERSON

4. Approaching sales from the wants and needs of others:

➢ Each line contains an effective and a less effective statement side by side.
Place a plus (+) next to the statements displaying effective persuasive skills.
Place a minus (−) next to the actions displaying less effective sales techniques.

___You need to understand that   ___This will fill your needs because

___If you were smarter you'd know that   ___What do you know about this so far

___By understanding the advantages you will want ___I need to sell you this because

___I know this is best for you because   ___You will feel this is best because

___People will enjoy watching your progress   ___I'll gain if you get this because

___Now I'm being totally honest when I tell you ___You've always been able to trust my

___Let me help you understand that   ___If you had been paying attention

___Will you buy this from me   ___You'll really love this because

___You'll appreciate the advantage of being able to ___This will cost you money but

___You'll only cry once, but you'll use it forever ___I know it's expensive, but

___You're friends will be so jealous because   ___People will think you're crazy, but

___Here's a great way to keep up with the   ___Others have said great things about

___Let's figure out a way for you to take this ___If you were listening you'd have known

___Do you want to buy a   ___You'll be so proud when you can show

(Add several more)

_____   _____

_____   _____

_____   _____

_____   _____

5. Understanding the Seven Cs of Sales...

➢ Whether you are a professional sales associate, university professor, laborer, student, stay-at-home mom, CEO, auto technician, or a warehouse worker, etc. you are involved in sales. You are perpetually attempting to empower others with the knowledge to comprehend the value of a product, service, activity, or an idea.

What if we look at an example of empowerment that I presented to a close friend a few years ago? We have spent many enjoyable years fly fishing for trout since the following discussion. My "sales pitch" went something like this.

➤ Fill in the "Seven Cs of Sales" (Courage, Connect, Challenge, Channel, Check, Confidence, and Celebrate) in the appropriate blanks.

"Hey Rich, I know that you feel safe being around the water (_____) and that you love to fish for salmon and steelhead. We have spent thousands of hours together chasing those elusive fish (_____). My sons and I have started fly fishing for trout. Talk about a tough way to deliver an offering to a fish while trying to convince the crafty critter that fur and feathers are a real meal (_____). We'd love to help you learn to cast a fly rod and get ya started tying flies. Because you learn so fast, I know you'll do just great! You can certainly borrow some of our fly fishing gear until you have time to go to the fly shop and select your own (_____). Fly fishing is a great value because once you buy your gear you're set forever. We row; consequently, there's no need to buy gas for the outboard, no bait because we use reusable flies, and the equipment lasts forever (_____). You'll absolutely love the quiet solitude and the beauty of the fishing spots we'll show you. If you thought you liked fishing for salmon and steelhead, just wait until that great big beautiful rainbow trout slurps in your dry fly and dances across the surface heading for parts unknown. We'd love to take you to the lake this Saturday. I'm sure glad you want to go (_____). I hope that your heart will be able to take the excitement; we'll have an absolute blast together (_____)!"

➤ Now include the use of the Seven Cs while writing a short note to a friend of yours explaining why they would like to pursue a hobby or activity that brings joy to your life.

_____

_____

_____

_____

_____

_____

_____

_____

_____

_____

_____

➤ Let's look at some of the details you covered in your "sales pitch" to your friend. What if we use the Seven *Cs* of Sales as a template for our analysis? Begin by placing the numbers 1–7 near the appropriate portion of your previous sales pitch. Circle the appropriate answer for each of the following questions.

1) Did you determine if your friend had the **courage** to be involved in the activity?

Yes   No

2) Did you **connect** by pointing out the value, benefits and advantages of the activity?

Yes   No

3) Did you describe the **challenges** involved in the endeavor?

Yes   No

4) Did you **channel** the information by explaining what needs to be done to be involved?

Yes   No

5) Will you be **checking** to ensure they understand the information?

Yes   No

6) Will your friend have **confidence** in the value, benefits, and advantages you have shown them?

Yes   No

7) Will you be able to **celebrate** the "close of the deal" because your friend accepted the "sales pitch?"

Yes   No

6. Comprehending that sales is teaching and teaching is sales:

➤ This will be hard to believe, but I remember when my wife and I heard about this new-fangled contraption called a microwave oven. We immediately ventured to an appliance store and reluctantly purchased one from a very fast talking, hard-working sales associate. Can you tell that was a long, long time ago?

Now that you have had some practice, try applying the Seven *Cs* of Sales to the following example. Imagine if someone were to ask you if they should purchase a microwave oven for the first time. What would you say to convince them to buy one? I am assuming it would be very easy for you to convince them of their need for one because you are probably thoroughly sold on the benefits of having a microwave. If this assumption is true, you have passed the first test of sales. You must be sold on the value of the product, idea, or service to be able to honestly convince others of its value. To sell them on their need for buying a microwave, you would simply list the features, advantages, and benefits that create the value they will receive by purchasing the unit.

You would probably explain how easy it is to operate the microwave, how fast it cooks the food, heats the beverages, thaws the frozen food, and warms up the leftovers, etc. You would probably tell them about all of the delicious, inexpensive, foods and snacks that can be prepared in a heartbeat. You would probably mention names of several friends who own one and how they would revolt if they had to live without it. Then you would probably explain how long the oven will last and the mere pennies it will cost per week for the convenience of preparing fantastic meals in a matter of seconds while stretching their food budget.

➤ Now it's your turn. Let's pretend that one of your friends has asked you if they should purchase a microwave oven. Remember one simple fact. They will appreciate and respect you more if you convince them to procure a product that will save them time and money!

"You should buy a microwave oven because

_____

_____

_____

_____

_____

_____

_____

_____

_____

_____

_____

_____

• CHECK

It's all about fulfilling the other person's wants and needs

➤ What would you like to strengthen in your Seven *Cs* of Sales.

_____

_____

_____

_____

_____

_____

_____

_____

• CONFIDENCE

"…leaders will be those who empower others." —Bill Gates

➤ List one or two goals on the accompanying forms that you would like to pursue to develop your skills of empowering others.

ASSESSING GOALS*

*List your goal(s) and assign a number from 0 to 10 (10 being high)
to each consideration of the goals setting process.*

GOALS ➤➤➤➤➤➤➤➤➤ _____   _____
(Primary Goal)   (Secondary Goal)

1. Level of need/passion	_____	_____
2. Level of desire to sacrifice	_____	_____
3. Level of research/planning	_____	_____
4. Level of action/skills	_____	_____
5. Ability to accept change	_____	_____
6. Ability to endure criticism	_____	_____
7. Available resources/assistance	_____	_____
8. Available time/energy	_____	_____
9. History of patience	_____	_____
10. History of commitment	_____	_____

Probability Index Total   _____   _____

Probability Index Scoring

90–100	Celebrate!	40–49	Should you reassess your goal?
80–89	Go for it!	30–39	Was your addition correct?
70–79	Have you analyzed obstacles?	20–29	Did you follow the directions?
60–69	Can you change anything?	10–19	Is it time for a reality check?
50–59	Is it worth the risk?	0–9	Possibly seek professional help?

*Greatness Only Awaits Labor…Staaaaaaaaaart!

_____

(CHAPTER TITLE)

_____

(GOAL/VISION/DREAM)

There is a need because:

_____

_____

The change, sacrifices and criticism that need to be addressed are:

_____

_____

_____

The assistance and resources that need to be procured are:

_____

_____

The history of patience and commitment has been:

_____

_____

In order to reach the goal I will:

_____

_____

_____

_____

_____

_____

_____

The beginning timeline is:

Set Goals	Planning	Implement	Completion?	Completed!
___/___/_____	___/___/_____	___/___/_____	___/___/_____	___/___/_____

The celebration plans are:

_____

_____

(CHAPTER TITLE)

(GOAL/VISION/DREAM)

There is a need because:

_____

_____

The change, sacrifices and criticism that need to be addressed are:

_____

_____

_____

The assistance and resources that need to be procured are:

_____

_____

The history of patience and commitment has been:

_____

_____

In order to reach the goal I will:

_____

_____

_____

_____

_____

_____

_____

The beginning timeline is:

Set Goals	Planning	Implement	Completion?	Completed!
___/___/_____	___/___/_____	___/___/_____	___/___/_____	___/___/_____

The celebration plans are:

_____

_____

Indicate the acronyms that will help you achieve your goals.

ACCEPT	All Circumstances Can Eventually Produce Truth
ACTIONS	Allowing Change Towards Improvement Offers Needed Success
ART	Always Representing Truth
BEAUTY	Beloved Experiences Always Useful To You
BORED	Bring On Remembrances Every Day
BORED	Bring On Recreation Every Day
BORED	Bring On Relationships Every Day
BROKE	Bountiful Revenue Only Keeps Escaping
CATALYST	Change Always Takes A Leader, You Should Try
CONFIDENCE	Changing Our Negative Fears Invites Delightful Experiences Never Considered Easy
COURAGE	Carefully Observing Underlying Risks Allows Goals to Evolve
DESIRE	Does Everyone Strive In Reaching Excellence
DREAMS	Desire Reflects Eventual Achievements Magically Secured
EASY	Everybody Always Says Yes
EMPOWER	Everyone Makes Pertinent Observations With Every Response
ENJOY	Everyone Now Journey Over Yonder
FEAR	Freezes Every Action; Reconsider
FEEL	Faith Eventually Elevates Love
FIRE	Free Individuals Real Effectively
FORGIVE	Freeing Our Resentment Garners Increased Value Every time
FUN	Forget Unnecessary Nonsense
GOALS	Goodness Only Awaits Labor . . . Start
GREAT	Golden Rule Elevates All Teams
HOBBY	Healthy Options Bring Back Youth
HOPE	Harnessing Optimism Produces Empowerment
HUMBLE	Hurry, Understand Me; Bragging Loses Everything
IDEA	Inspiration Deserves Everyone's Attention
IMPROVE	Individuals Make Progress Rewarding Our Valiant Efforts
JOB	Just Over Broke
JOYS	Just Open Your Soul
JOYS	Just Offer Your Spirit
LEARN	Love Education, Achieve Respect Now
LIE	Losers Intentionally Exaggerate
LOVE	Lights On, Very Empowering
MEMORIES	Most Events Make Our Recollections Youthful
MESSAGE	Making Every Statement Significant, Allowing Goodness to Enter
MIND	Magical Insights Now Develop
MONEY	Move Over Negativism, Enter Yes-man
MUSIC	Mankind's Ultimate Study In Creation
PASSION	People Always Seek Success If Opportunity's Noble
PEP	Positive Energy People
PLAN	Please Learn All Necessities

POSITIVE	Please Offer Sincere Insights To Instill Values Effectively
PRIDE	People Respect Individuals Delivering Excellence
PROFITS	Providing Revenue Opportunities Fulfills Individual Tasks Successfully
SALES	Sincere Attitudes Launch Everyone Successfully
SHY	Sure Hurts You
SORRY	Success Often Requires Rescinding Yourself
SOUL	Source Of Unconditional Love
TEACH	Teaming Eventually Activates Correct Habits
TEAM	Tolerance Empowers All Members
TRUTH	To Respectfully Uncover The Honesty
TRY	To Respect Yourself
WORRY	Wickedness Only Result'n Resentment, Y'know
YELL	You Eventually Lose Love

EMPOWERMENT

CharacterConstructionCompany.com

ACROSS

4 Bring On Remembrances Every Day
5 People Always Seek Success If Opportunity's Noble
9 To Respectfully Uncover The Honesty
11 Hurry Understand Me Bragging Loses Everything
16 Allowing Change Towards Improvement Offers Needed Success
17 Making Every Statement Significant Allowing Goodness to Enter
18 Magical Insights Now Develop
20 Sincere Attitudes Launch Everyone Successfully
21 Healthy Options Bring Back Youth
22 Lights On Very Empowering
24 Just Offer Your Spirit
25 Bring On Recreation Every Day
27 Everyone Makes Pertinent Observations With Every Response
30 To Respect Yourself
32 Success Often Requires Rescinding Yourself
33 Positive Energy People
35 Desire Reflects Eventual Achievements Magically Secured
38 You Eventually Lose Love
41 Harnessing Optimism Produces Empowerment
44 Losers Intentionally Exaggerate
45 Freeing Our Resentment Garners Increased Value Everytime
46 Always Representing Truth
47 All Circumstances Can Eventually Produce Truth
49 Freezes Every Action Reconsider
50 Forget Unnecessary Nonsense

DOWN

1 Just Open Your Soul
2 Teaming Eventually Activates Correct Habits
3 Just Over Broke
5 Please Offer Sincere Insights To Instill Values Effectively
6 People Respect Individuals Delivering Excellence
7 Sure Hurts You
8 Golden Rule Empowers All Teams
10 Does Everyone Strive In Reaching Excellence
12 Move Over Negativism Enter Yesman
13 Carefully Observing Underlying Risks Allows Goals to Evolve
14 Individuals Make Progress Rewarding Our Valiant Efforts
15 Change Always Takes A Leader You Should Try
19 Wickedness Only Results'n Resentment Y'Know
23 Changing Our Negative Fears Invites Delightful Experiences Never Considered Easy
25 Beloved Experiences Always Useful To You
26 Everybody Always Says Yes
28 Most Events Make Our Recollections Include Everlasting Success
29 Tolerance Empowers All Members
31 Goodness Only Awaits Labor Start
34 Providing Revenue Opportunities Fulfills Individual Tasks Successfully
36 Everyone Now Journey Over Yonder
37 Source Of Unconditional Love
39 Mankind's Ultimate Study In Creation
40 Inspiration Deserves Everyone's Attention
42 Bring On Relationships Every Day
43 Love Education Achieve Respect Now
48 Please Learn All Necessities

EMPOWERMENT

Find the words in the grid. When you are done, the unused letters in the grid will spell out a hidden message. Pick them out from left to right, top line to bottom line. Words can go horizontally, vertically and diagonally in all eight directions.

```
L E A D E R D M S T P O S I T I V E E S
E M G P O A W R U R R E R E V O L M E E
O T H R E S E R E S A U S Z N R P L G J
G X M H E T E D Y A I E T K H O A A H H
C N A L P A S I I J M C F H W S R M O Y
E L B M U H T Y R R F S M E H U L R B R
S R J L R E M W L O X M R O O V T B B T
P H M E H Y D A Q A M N P C E Q X O Y N
A M Y A R T N I E N T E Z E V S Y R P C
S D E R O B S A R T E A M V I O T E R L
S M O N M N T B W P G R C O G R P D R E
I W P L O R C R T R A M M R R R V D B C
O T Y I Y O J N E R S L D P O Y N O M N
N Z T J O Y S L A J S M F M F I R L S E
L C M O N E Y Y S T E B M I M E I O T D
A J D Y E L L B Y P M J E G D E U F I I
L K K V D E S I R E V H O A K L F M F F
M Z C T B D P L L C T B Y Y U N D N O N
R F M O N Y N T H C A E T N S T U L R O
Y F J G O A L S M A T L T T N F Y T P C
```

www.CharacterConstructionCompany.com

ACCEPT	COURAGE	GOALS	JOYS	PASSION	SOUL
ACTIONS	DESIRE	GREAT	LEARN	PEP	TEACH
ART	DREAMS	HOBBY	LIE	PLAN	TEAM
BEAUTY	EASY	HOPE	LOVE	POSITIVE	TRUTH
BORED	EMPOWER	HUMBLE	MEMORIES	PRIDE	TRY
BORED	ENJOY	IDEA	MESSAGE	PROFIT	WORRY
BORED	FEAR	IMPROVE	MIND	SALES	YELL
CATALYST	FORGIVE	JOB	MONEY	SHY	
CONFIDENCE	FUN	JOYS	MUSIC	SORRY	

RELATIONSHIPS
Realizing Every Love Allows Truth In Our Normal Situations,
Helping Individuals Proclaim Self-Worth

• CONNECT
Learning to live, love, and let go

Learning how to _____ (**L**ove **E**ducation; **A**chieve **R**espect **N**ow) to be

_____ (**R**econsidering **E**very **S**ituation **P**revents

Occasional **N**egative **S**tandards **I**nfluencing **B**ehavior **L**eading to **E**xtremes) for our actions helps

us feel we _____ (**B**eautiful **E**ncounters **L**et **O**pportunities **N**ow **G**row),

we are_____, (**N**otice **E**veryone's **E**steem **D**evelop **E**ach **D**ay), and we find

_____ (**L**ights **O**n **V**ery **E**mpowering) in our lives. Throughout life's journey we

learn to _____ (**T**o **R**espect **Y**ourself) to _____ (**A**ll **C**ircumstances

Can **E**ventually **P**roduce **T**ruth) the danger of being _____ (**L**ove **O**nly **N**eed

Escape, **L**ife **Y**earns) because of relationships ending and facing _____

(**G**ranting **R**espect, **I**nspiring **E**verlasting **F**riendships).

• CHALLENGE
Learning the intricacies of relationships

1. Learning how to learn:

➢ List things that are easy for you to learn and things that are challenging for you to learn. You might consider classes in school, interests, hobbies, relationships, etc.

EASY TO LEARN	CHALLENGING TO LEARN
a._____	a._____
b._____	b._____
c._____	c._____
d._____	d._____

2. Being responsible for your actions:

➤ List your involvement with the things on the previous listings. Are you pursuing the activities that have been easy for you to learn? What has become of the things that have been hard for you to learn?

OUTCOMES OF EASY TO LEARN	OUTCOMES OF HARD TO LEARN
a._____	a._____
b._____	b._____
c._____	c._____
d._____	d._____

3. Learning keys in developing relationships:

➤ If relationships are the most important aspect of your life, would it follow that we should perpetually learn how to successfully develop them? The heading for this section could be the title for this entire book. You would probably agree the entire book is an exercise in how to get along with yourself and with those around you.

➤ Let's imagine you are visiting a person you would like to begin a friendship with. Select which statements would be the most appropriate. There is an appropriate statement and a less appropriate statement on each line. Place a plus (+) by what you would hope they would say to you and a minus (−) next to what you would consider an inappropriate statement.

____Hi, my name's...what's yours?   ____Do you want to know me?

____I've heard questionable things about you.   ____I've heard lots of great things.

____How do you like to spend your free time?   ____Are you interested in my . . . ?

____I work at . . . and I make . . .   ____What do you do during the day?

____I'm sorry you had to grow up here.   ____Where did you grow up?

____Where did you go to school?   ____I think the best school is . . .

____What do you think of . . .   ____In my opinion, I think . . .

____Can you believe how stupid those . . .   ____Do you think it's fair that . . .

____What is your favorite place to visit?   ____I can't stand it . . . because . . .

____Do you like your . . .   ____I don't like mine because . . .

_____   _____

_____   _____

_____   _____

Did you mark a plus on only the positive statements?

      _____Yes

      _____No

Have you made positive and negative statements similar to the preceding list?

      _____Yes

      _____No

Do you realize the detrimental effect of the negative statements?

      _____Yes

      _____No

4. Understanding the importance of belonging, being needed and being loved:

➢ To belong to an organization means that you (check one):

    _____a. are a member of a team, group, family, supporter of a cause, fan, etc.
    _____b. proclaimed your allegiance to the group, school, company, team, etc.
    _____c. agreed to the stipulations of membership.
    _____d. feel a sense of inclusion.
    _____e. all of the above.
    _____f. all of the above.

➢ To feel needed means that you have (check one):

    _____a. accepted something from an individual or organization.
    _____b. received praise for getting lucky.
    _____c. shared some of your time, gifts, and talents with others.
    _____d. all of the above.
    _____e. none of the above.

➢ To feel loved means that you (check one):

    _____a. have shared your time with others.
    _____b. have shared your gifts with others.
    _____c. have shared your talents with others.
    _____d. have been accepted on an extraordinary emotional level by others.
    _____e. possibly all of the above.
    _____f. possibly all of the above.

5. Learning the four ingredients in relationships:

➤ Select and circle four ingredients contained in relationships.

    Comfort   Goals   Mystery   Timing

6. Understanding a simple method of viewing all relationships:

➤ What were the last two or three sentences you said to a person
when you saw them for the very last time?

"_____

_____

_____

_____"

7. Facing grief:

➤ Do you feel that the most difficult part of relationships is accepting the loss of loved ones?
(check one)

_____Yes

_____No

• CHANNEL

Learning to change or solidify our responses

1. Learning how to learn:

➤ List, in order, what is easiest for you to learn. Try to determine if is easier for you to learn in a
positive environment or a negative environment.

SKILL/KNOWLEDGE	**CHECK ONE**	
HAS BEEN EASY TO LEARN	**POSITIVE ENVIRONMENT**	**NEGATIVE ENVIRONMENT**
_____	_____	_____
_____	_____	_____
_____	_____	_____
_____	_____	_____

SKILL/KNOWLEDGE	**CHECK ONE**	
HAS BEEN DIFFICULT TO LEARN	**POSITIVE ENVIRONMENT**	**NEGATIVE ENVIRONMENT**
_____	_____	_____
_____	_____	_____
_____	_____	_____
_____	_____	_____

2. Being responsible for your actions:

➢ Fill in some of the consequences for the following actions. To assist you, a partial listing of potential consequences follows this activity.

ACTIONS	**POTENTIAL CONSEQUENCES**
1. Lying	_____
2. Bullying	_____
3. Spreading rumors	_____
4. Teasing	_____
5. Stealing	_____
6. Cheating	_____
7. Anger	_____

8. Substances abuse _____

9. Overeating _____

10. Eating disorders _____

11. Carelessness _____

12. Neglecting rules _____

13. Neglecting laws _____

14. Disrespecting _____

15. Gossiping _____

16. Abusing alcohol _____

17. Smoking _____

18. Fighting _____

19. Violence _____

20. _____ _____

21. _____ _____

22. _____ _____

➤ Place a check mark by the potential consequences of inappropriate actions that would best end the following sentence.

"The potential consequences for the above actions can result in the loss of _____."

__respect	__privileges	__freedom	__job	__activities
__money	__reputation	__friends	__trust	__confidence
__physical health	__abilities	__breathing	__peace	__athleticism
__coordination	__opportunities	__mind	__skills	__mental health
__talent	__pride	__happiness	__family	__enthusiasm
__credibility	__motivation	__creativity	__welcome	__joy
__hobbies	__sanity	__fun	__safety	__sight
__sense of smell	__belonging	__spiritualism	__soul	__love
__appearance	__time	__speech	__sleep	__money
__peace of mind	__future	__life	__emotional stability	

_____   _____   _____   _____

_____   _____   _____   _____

➢ Place a check mark by the potential consequences of inappropriate actions that would best end the following sentence.

"The potential consequences for inappropriate actions can result in _____."

__physical illness	__incessant cough	__fear	__intimidation
__hospitalization	__rehabilitation	__handcuffs	__injury
__murder	__disease	__arrest	__jail
__accidents	__ridicule	__overweight	__obesity
__incarceration	__legal citations	__financial fines	__abuse
__manslaughter	__assault	__rejection	__addiction
__alcoholism	__burned bridges	__ended relationships	__mental illness

_____   _____   _____   _____

_____   _____   _____   _____

3. Learning keys in developing relationships:

➢ Think of someone you would like to develop or rekindle a relationship with. Check the important points that will help you in developing and maintaining that relationship.
Check the words that best end the following sentence.

"My relationships will be more successful if I will be _____."

IMPORTANT CONSIDERATION   **ADDITIONAL CONSIDERATIONS**

__more understanding   _____

__more forgiving   _____

__more patient   _____

__more kind   _____

__nonjudgmental   _____

__more complimentary   _____

__more tolerant   _____

__more loving   _____

__more giving   _____

__less taking   _____

__less demanding   _____

__realistic with expectations   _____

__more accepting   _____

__more truthful   _____

___less controlling　　　　　_____

___less critical　　　　　　　_____

___more humorous　　　　　_____

___more helpful　　　　　　_____

___more generous　　　　　_____

___more attractive　　　　　_____

___not expecting perfection　_____

4.　Understanding the importance of belonging, being needed, and being loved:

➤ List the family, teams, groups, schools, clubs, community organizations, companies, etc., that you have belonged or currently belong to.

BELONG TO	BELONG TO
_____	_____
_____	_____
_____	_____

➤ Describe how your talents, time, and gifts have given you a feeling of being needed by organizations.

GROUP	NEEDED FOR
_____	_____
_____	_____
_____	_____

➤ Describe how your talents, time, and gifts have given you a feeling of being loved by some of those organizations.

GROUP	LOVED BECAUSE
_____	_____
_____	_____
_____	_____
_____	_____
_____	_____

➤ Considering those experiences, list some people and their actions you would like to forgive for something they did to <u>offend you</u> (initials are fine).

PERSON   **ACTION**

_____   _____

_____   _____

_____   _____

➤ Considering those experiences, list the people that you would like to have forgive you for <u>your actions</u> (initials are fine).

PERSON   **ACTION**

_____   _____

_____   _____

_____   _____

5. Learning the four ingredients in relationships:

➤ List what you feel are the essential considerations and traits under each key ingredient in a relationship with an associate, a close friend, spouse, partner, family member, or a "person of your dreams."

COMFORT

_____

_____

_____

_____

_____

GOALS

_____

_____

_____

_____

_____

MYSTERY

_____

_____

_____

_____

_____

TIMING

_____

_____

_____

_____

_____

➤ Let's take a look at learning how to assess relationships. Complete the following "Rating Relationships Form."

RATING RELATIONSHIPS

List people you are currently experiencing a relationship/friendship with and assign a number from 0 to 10 (10 being high) to each consideration of the relationship to help quantify the value of those relationships.

PERSON ➤➤➤➤➤➤➤ _____ _____
(person's name)   (person's name)

1. Level of comfort/respect	_____	_____
2. Level of honesty/trust	_____	_____
3. Supporting common goals	_____	_____
4. Common interests/activities	_____	_____
5. Level of mystery/communication	_____	_____
6. Atmosphere of compassion	_____	_____
7. Availability of quality time	_____	_____
8. History of commitment	_____	_____
9. Capacity for patience/forgiveness	_____	_____
10. Appropriate appearance	_____	_____

Relationship Value Total   _____   _____

Depth of Relationship Rating

90–100 . . . Precious Treasure!

80–89 . . . . Enjoy the Benefits!

70–79 . . . . Exercise Caution!

60–69 . . . . Can you communicate?

50–59 . . . . Is it worth the risk?

40–49 . . . Should you reconsider motives?

30–39 . . . Is something WAY out of balance?

20–29 . . . Do you understand why others criticize?

10–19 . . . Considered changing your phone number?

0–9 . . . Moving without a forwarding address?

6. Understanding a simple method of viewing all relationships:

➤ Think of the last time you were unhappy with your final farewell to someone. Do you wish you could have another chance to talk with that person? What would you have said if you knew that would have been your last chance to visit with that individual? If your conversation would have been different, please write what you wish you would have said.

"_____

_____

_____

_____

_____ "

7. Facing grief:

➤ What helps you endure the loss of a loved one?
Please place a plus (+) on the statements that might help you face losing a loved one. Place a minus (−) on what you would like to avoid.

____Accepting the departed is at peace

____Understanding that feelings of guilt are a normal part of grieving

____Repeatedly saying "If only I coulda, shoulda, woulda"

____Remembering that respect was displayed

____Understanding that personal strife is part of being human

____Realizing there were things I should have said

____Occasional crying

____Uncontrollable crying

____Transferring love to others

____Viewing the departed

____Realizing that leaving life on earth is the one price we pay for living

____Reliving pleasant memories

____Understanding that I should have been more aware

____I would have spent more time with the person if . . .

____Understanding that denial is a natural defense mechanism

____Forgetting hurtful memories

____Controlling the desire to perpetually dwell on the loss

_____Enduring criticism regarding displaying grief

_____Laughing about the humor we shared

_____I wish I would have spent more time sharing conversations about the…

_____Withdrawing from friends and family

_____Researching and studying the topic of grief

_____Discussing the departed with mutual friends

_____Comprehending that accepting the reality of loss is essential

_____Practicing faith

_____Understanding that anger is a normal reaction in losing a loved one

_____Remembering that grief is a journey, not the destination

_____Being involved with support groups

_____Forgiving myself for any hurt I inflicted

_____Visiting the resting place

_____Concentrating more on developing current friendships

_____Sharing my feelings with others

_____Continuing to celebrate their special occasions

_____Seeking guidance from their memories

_____Celebrating the memories of time together

➤ Explain what you have discovered that best helps you "live through" losing a loved one.

_____

_____

_____

_____

_____

- **CHECK**

    A measure of a successful life is developing a handful of close friends,
    of which, you are the closest.

- **CONFIDENCE**

    If you were going to die soon and you had time to do something for somebody,

    What would you do?
    Who would you do it for?
    Why are you waiting?

➤ List a primary goal and potentially a secondary goal on the following forms you would like to pursue in developing and preserving relationships.

ASSESSING GOALS*

*List your goal(s) and assign a number from 0 to 10 (10 being high)
to each consideration of the goals setting process.*

GOALS ➤➤➤➤➤➤➤➤➤ _____   _____

                                            (Primary Goal)   (Secondary Goal)

	Primary Goal	Secondary Goal
1. Level of need/passion	_____	_____
2. Level of desire to sacrifice	_____	_____
3. Level of research/planning	_____	_____
4. Level of action/skills	_____	_____
5. Ability to accept change	_____	_____
6. Ability to endure criticism	_____	_____
7. Available resources/assistance	_____	_____
8. Available time/energy	_____	_____
9. History of patience	_____	_____
10. History of commitment	_____	_____

Probability Index Total   _____   _____

Probability Index Scoring

90–100 . . . . . . Celebrate!   40–49 . . . . . . Should you reassess your goal?
80–89 . . . . Go for it!   30–39 . . . . . . Was your addition correct?
70–79 . . . . Have you analyzed obstacles?   20–29 . . . . . . Did you follow the directions?
60–69 . . . . Can you change anything?   10–19 . . . . . . Is it time for a reality check?
50–59 . . . . Is it worth the risk?   0–9 . . . . . . Possibly seek professional help?

*Greatness Only Awaits Labor…Staaaaaaaaaart!

_____

(CHAPTER TITLE)

_____

(GOAL/VISION/DREAM)

There is a need because:

_____

_____

The change, sacrifices and criticism that need to be addressed are:

_____

_____

_____

The assistance and resources that need to be procured are:

_____

_____

The history of patience and commitment has been:

_____

_____

In order to reach the goal I will:

_____

_____

_____

_____

_____

_____

_____

The beginning timeline is:

Set Goals	Planning	Implement	Completion?	Completed!
___/___/____	___/___/____	___/___/____	___/___/____	___/___/____

The celebration plans are:

_____

_____

_____

(CHAPTER TITLE)

_____

(GOAL/VISION/DREAM)

There is a need because:

_____

_____

The change, sacrifices and criticism that need to be addressed are:

_____

_____

_____

The assistance and resources that need to be procured are:

_____

_____

The history of patience and commitment has been:

_____

_____

In order to reach the goal I will:

_____

_____

_____

_____

_____

_____

The beginning timeline is:

Set Goals	Planning	Implement	Completion?	Completed!
___/___/_____	___/___/_____	___/___/_____	___/___/_____	___/___/_____

The celebration plans are:

_____

_____

Indicate the acronyms that will help you achieve your goals.

ABUSE	All Beings Underestimate Some Eventualities
ACCEPT	All Circumstances Can Eventually Produce Truth
ACTIONS	Allowing Change Towards Improvement Offers Needed Success
BAD	Bullies Always Destroy
BELONG	Beautiful Encounters Let Opportunities Now Grow
BOSS	Big On Securing Success
COMFORT	Consolation Often Means Forgetting Our Realities Today
CRY	Caring Reveals You
DEMAND	Do Everything Management Asks, No Discussion
FACT	Finding Actual Circumstances True
FREEDOM	Forget Restrictions, Enjoy Every Delightful Opportunistic Moment
FUN	Forget Unnecessary Nonsense
GRIEF	Granting Respect, Inspiring Everlasting Friendships
HEART	Help Everyone Achieve Respect Today
KWIK	Kill With Instant Kindness
LEARN	Love Education; Achieve Respect Now
LIFE	Love Is For Everyone
LONELY	Love Only Need Escape; Life Yearns
LOVE	Lights On, Very Empowering
NEEDED	Notice Everyone's Esteem Develop Each Day
NICE	Never Insult, Compliment Everyone
RESPONSIBLE	Reconsidering Every Situation Prevents Occasional Negative Standards Influencing Behavior Leading to Extremes
SMILE	Sure Makes It Lots Easier
SOUL	Source Of Unconditional Love
STRESS	Some Think Redirecting Energy Saves Sanity
TRAGEDY	Terrible Results Accentuate Grief, Everyone Deliriously Yearns
TRY	To Respect Yourself

RELATIONSHIPS

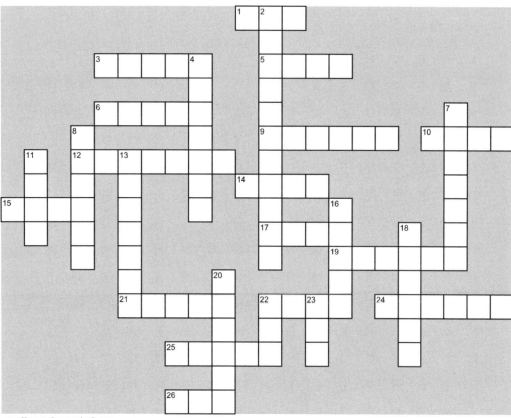

www.CharacterConstructionCompany.com

ACROSS

1 To Respect Yourself

3 Granting Respect, Inspiring Everlasting Friendships

5 Source Of Unconditional Love

6 All Beings Underestimate Some Eventualities

9 Notice Everyone's Esteem Develop Each Day

10 Big On Securing Success

12 Terrible Results Accentuate Grief; Everyone Deliriously Yearns

14 Never Insult Compliment Everyone

15 Love Is For Everyone

17 Lights On Very Empowering

19 All Circumstances Can Eventually Produce Truth

21 Sure Makes It Lots Easier

22 Finding Actual Circumstances True

24 Love Only Need Escape Life Yearns

25 Love Education Achieve Respect Now

26 Bullies Always Destroy

DOWN

2 Reconsidering Every Situation Prevents Occasional Negative Standards Influencing Behavior Leading to Extremes

4 Forget Restrictions Enjoy Every Delightful Opportunistic Moment

7 Consolation Often Means Forgetting Our Realities Today

8 Some Think Redirecting Energy Saves Sanity

11 Kill With Instant Kindness

13 Allowing Change Towards Improvement Offers Needed Success

16 Help Everyone Achieve Respect Today

18 Beautiful Encounters Let Opportunities Now Grow

20 Do Everything Management Asks No Discussion

22 Forget Unnecessary Nonsense

23 Caring Reveals You

RELATIONSHIPS

Find the words in the grid. When you are done, the unused letters in the grid will spell out a hidden message. Pick them out from left to right, top line to bottom line. Words can go horizontally, vertically and diagonally in all eight directions.

```
L N O V R E S P O N S I B L E E I
S N E F O S R T R O F M O C E V E
R I Y E M O N E E A C T I O N S D
P C X I D W G S M T K K X G P H Q
R E L T V E Z U K P Q N Q L C Q R
D E K F T E D B B D B R K I W K C
R W B L Y F W A Y O T L D L U O S
M P F T G I G N S R K Y N L H M R
V P C U X L M S L M C X A L T N Z
N A T C N R G N B R B C M L G K Y
F L R F R E E D O M E P E W M L D
G P K Y S Y Y M T L N D B T H E
R V F F V L S L P Z O Z R N E N G
I N Z L E R V E B Y N K J A M L A
E J J N V R C V R B G M R D E G R
F D O M X C X T K T A T H N C L T
L L K Q A B L O V E S D D M F N R
```

www.CharacterConstructionCompany.com

ABUSE	FACT	LOVE
ACCEPT	FREEDOM	NEEDED
ACTIONS	FUN	NICE
BAD	GRIEF	RESPONSIBLE
BELONG	HEART	SMILE
BOSS	KWIK	SOUL
COMFORT	LEARN	STRESS
CRY	LIFE	TRAGEDY
DEMAND	LONELY	TRY

INSPIRE

Individuals Need Support Philosophically
In Reaching Expectations

• CONNECT

To understand the importance of faith in reaching goals

Possessing _____ (**F**orget **A**ll **I**nsecurities **T**rust **H**ope) gives us _____

(**H**arnessing **O**ptimism **P**roduces **E**mpowerment) of nourishing our _____ (**S**ource **O**f

Unconditional **L**ove) throughout our _____ (**L**ove **I**s **F**or **E**veryone). Offering

an _____ (**I**nspiration **D**eserves **E**veryone's **A**ttention) can _____ (**I**ndividuals

Need **S**upport **P**hilosophically **I**n **R**eaching **E**xpectations) others to find _____

(**R**ecognizing **E**veryone's **S**trengths **P**roduces **E**xceptional **C**aring **T**eams) and overcome feelings of

_____ (**G**iving **U**p **I**nequities **L**eaves **T**rust) and fears of being _____

(**L**ove **O**nly **N**eed **E**scape, **L**ife **Y**earns).

• CHALLENGE

To discover ingredients that illuminate life's plan

1. Comprehending the mystical comforting powers of music (this one's really easy):

➢ List several musical selections that you enjoy listening to.

MUSICAL SELECTIONS	PERFORMERS
_____	_____
_____	_____
_____	_____
_____	_____
_____	_____

2. Discovering the rules of life:

➤ List some of the sources that you seek out to discover the rules for your life.

_____   _____

_____   _____

3. Searching for avenues to discover personal happiness:

➤ List people (initials will be fine), places, and things that bring you happiness.

PEOPLE	PLACES	THINGS
_____	_____	_____
_____	_____	_____
_____	_____	_____

4. Avoiding negative situations:

➤ List the people (initials will be fine), places, and things that you attempt to avoid because of the negative effects they have on you.

PEOPLE	PLACES	THINGS
_____	_____	_____
_____	_____	_____
_____	_____	_____

5. Believing in personal control:

➤ List the level of control that you have over some elements in your life-as an example, the weather, friends, food, etc.

NO CONTROL	SOME CONTROL	TOTAL CONTROL
_____	_____	_____
_____	_____	_____
_____	_____	_____

6. Witnessing positive results of sharing goodness:

➤ List three people who have been your positive role models and how they have inspired you.

PEOPLE	INFLUENCE
_____	_____
_____	_____
_____	_____

• CHANNEL
Living by our plan and sharing goodness

1. Comprehending the mystical comforting powers of music:

➤ List several of your favorite pieces of music and describe how they affect your state of mind.

MUSICAL SELECTIONS	STATE OF MIND
_____	_____
_____	_____
_____	_____
_____	_____
_____	_____

2. Discovering the rules of life:

➤ What music, books, periodicals, speakers, organizations, etc., provide an inspiration for you to establish and abide by your self-imposed "rules of life?"

_____	_____
_____	_____
_____	_____
_____	_____

3. Searching for avenues to discover personal happiness:

➢ Complete this statement.

"I experience the most joy in life when I _____

_____

_____

_____ "

4. Avoiding negative situations:

➢ Complete this statement.

"My world would be perfect if _____

_____

_____

_____

_____ "

5. Believing in personal control:

➢ I understand that HOPE means **H**arnessing **O**ptimism **P**roduces **E**mpowerment and that I have control over many elements of my life. I can learn to be more empowered if I practice more control over the following.

WHO (PEOPLE)	WHERE (PLACES)	WHAT (THINGS)	WHY (RULES)
_____	_____	_____	_____
_____	_____	_____	_____
_____	_____	_____	_____

6. Witnessing positive results of sharing goodness:

➢ List the people and/or numbers of people who have followed your influence because you have been an inspiration for them.

PEOPLE	INFLUENCE
_____	_____
_____	_____
_____	_____

• CHECK

"Genius is one percent inspiration, ninety-nine percent perspiration."
—Thomas Edison

"Through this chapter I have learned that _____

_____

_____

_____

_____

_____

_____ "

• CONFIDENCE

"The ultimate measure of a man is not where he stands in moments of comfort, but where he stands at times of challenge and controversy." —Martin Luther King, Jr.

➤ List the goals for inspiring yourself and/or your acquaintances on the following forms.

ASSESSING GOALS*

*List your goal(s) and assign a number from 0 to 10 (10 being high)
to each consideration of the goals setting process.*

GOALS ➤➤➤➤➤➤➤➤➤ _____   _____
(Primary Goal)   (Secondary Goal)

	Primary Goal	Secondary Goal
1. Level of need/passion	_____	_____
2. Level of desire to sacrifice	_____	_____
3. Level of research/planning	_____	_____
4. Level of action/skills	_____	_____
5. Ability to accept change	_____	_____
6. Ability to endure criticism	_____	_____
7. Available resources/assistance	_____	_____
8. Available time/energy	_____	_____
9. History of patience	_____	_____
10. History of commitment	_____	_____

Probability Index Total   _____   _____

Probability Index Scoring

90–100 . . . . . . Celebrate!   40–49 . . . . . . Should you reassess your goal?

80–89 . . . . Go for it!   30–39 . . . . . . Was your addition correct?

70–79 . . . . Have you analyzed obstacles?   20–29 . . . . . . Did you follow the directions?

60–69 . . . . Can you change anything?   10–19 . . . . . . Is it time for a reality check?

50–59 . . . . Is it worth the risk?   0–9 . . . . . . Possibly seek professional help?

*Greatness Only Awaits Labor…Staaaaaaaaart!

_____
(CHAPTER TITLE)

_____
(GOAL/VISION/DREAM)

There is a need because:

_____

_____

The change, sacrifices and criticism that need to be addressed are:

_____

_____

_____

The assistance and resources that need to be procured are:

_____

_____

The history of patience and commitment has been:

_____

_____

In order to reach the goal I will:

_____

_____

_____

_____

_____

_____

The beginning timeline is:

Set Goals	Planning	Implement	Completion?	Completed!
___/___/____	___/___/____	___/___/____	___/___/____	___/___/____

The celebration plans are:

_____

_____

_____

(CHAPTER TITLE)

_____

(GOAL/VISION/DREAM)

There is a need because:

_____

_____

The change, sacrifices and criticism that need to be addressed are:

_____

_____

_____

The assistance and resources that need to be procured are:

_____

_____

The history of patience and commitment has been:

_____

_____

In order to reach the goal I will:

_____

_____

_____

_____

_____

_____

_____

The beginning timeline is:

Set Goals	Planning	Implement	Completion?	Completed!
___/___/_____	___/___/_____	___/___/_____	___/___/_____	___/___/_____

The celebration plans are:

_____

_____

Indicate the acronyms that will help you achieve your goals.

BEST	Beautiful Endeavors Seem Terrific
BLESSED	Bountiful Love Endures Scorn 'n Sadness, Enters the Deity
CARING	Citizens Always Respond with Integrity, Not Greed
FAITH	Forget All Insecurities; Trust Hope
GUILT	Giving Up Inequities Leaves Trust
HAPPY	Have All the Peace 'n Pleasure Ya want
HOPE	Harnessing Optimism Produces Empowerment
IDEA	Inspiration Deserves Everyone's Attention
KIND	Keep It Nice, Dear
LIFE	Love Is For Everyone
LONELY	Love Only Need Escape; Life Yearns
LOVE	Lights On, Very Empowering
MEANING	Making Every Action Naturally Include Noble Goals
MUSIC	Mankind's Ultimate Study In Creation
PLAN	Please Learn All Necessities
POWER	People Only Want Elevated Respect
PRAYER	Powerful Resources Await Your Every Request
REALITIES	Realizing Events, Accepting Life's Inequities Teaches Individuals Everlasting Structure
RESPECT	Recognizing Everyone's Strengths Produces Exceptional Caring Teams
RULES	Regulating Us Leads Everyone to Success
SOUL	Source Of Unconditional Love
TRY	To Respect Yourself

INSPIRE

www.CharacterConstructionCompany.com

ACROSS

2 Please Learn All Necessities
5 Harnessing Optimism Produces Empowerment
7 Regulating Us Leads Everyone to Success
9 Powerful Resources Await Your Every Request
11 Love Only Need Escape Life Yearns
12 Keep It Nice Dear
14 Mankind's Ultimate Study In Creation
16 Realizing Events Accepting Life's Inequities Teaches Individuals Everlasting Structure
17 Recognizing Everyone's Strengths Produces Exceptional Caring Teams
18 Giving Up Inequities Leaves Trust

DOWN

1 Citizens Always Respond with Integrity Not Greed
2 People Only Want Elevated Respect
3 Source Of Unconditional Love
4 Bountiful Love Endures Scorn'n Sadness Enters the Deity
5 Have All the Peace 'n Pleasure Y'want
6 To Respect Yourself
8 Making Every Action Naturally Include Noble Goals
10 Love Is For Everyone
13 Beautiful Endeavors Seem Terrific
15 Inspiration Deserves Everyone's Attention
19 Lights On Very Empowering

132

INSPIRE

Find the words in the grid. When you are done, the unused letters in the grid will spell out a hidden message. Pick them out from left to right, top line to bottom line. Words can go horizontally, vertically and diagonally in all eight directions.

```
H  A  R  N  E  S  G  R  E  W  O  P  S
M  S  I  P  N  G  Y  U  O  P  T  I  E
E  M  L  I  S  L  H  M  I  D  P  L  L
A  A  R  O  E  O  R  D  E  L  U  D  U
N  U  R  N  P  E  C  S  N  O  T  H  R
I  M  O  E  S  E  S  S  I  E  A  T
N  L  U  P  Y  E  L  O  V  E  K  P  S
G  M  E  S  L  A  P  T  R  Y  O  P  E
W  C  E  B  I  R  R  M  E  E  N  Y  B
T  T  T  Q  N  C  Y  P  L  F  G  V  H
P  H  C  A  R  I  N  G  P  I  D  Z  K
A  E  D  I  L  J  K  G  D  L  T  F  T
D  M  J  V  S  E  I  T  I  L  A  E  R
```

www.CharacterConstructionCompany.com

BEST	KIND	POWER
BLESSED	LIFE	PRAYER
CARING	LONELY	REALITIES
GUILT	LOVE	RESPECT
HAPPY	MEANING	RULES
HOPE	MUSIC	SOUL
IDEA	PLAN	TRY

SELF-WORTH
Securing Esteem Lessens Fear; Working Offers Respect, Triggering Happiness

• CONNECT
Recognizing personal value

Hopefully we can _____ (**L**ove **E**ducation, **A**chieve **R**espect **N**ow) to _____ (**B**ountiful **E**xperiences **L**oved **I**f **E**veryone **V**isualizes **E**ventualities) in ourselves by developing a sense of _____ (**P**eople **R**espect **I**ndividuals **D**elivering **E**xcellence) based on _____ (**H**appiness **A**waits **R**elentless **D**esire) _____ (**W**e **O**nly **R**espect **K**indness) and doing the _____ (**R**especting **I**ntegrity **G**rants **H**onor **T**oday) thing. Let's _____ (**H**arnessing **O**ptimism **P**roduces **E**mpowerment) that _____ (**D**o **R**esults **U**ltimately **G**uarantee **S**uccess) and _____ (**A**lways **L**imit **C**onsumption **O**ften **H**inders **O**ur **L**ives) don't become _____ (**H**ow **A**ll **B**eings **I**mprint **T**raits) of getting _____ (**H**elping **I**ndividuals **G**et **H**appy). Some people will need to not _____ (**A**ll **B**eings **U**nderestimate **S**ome **E**ventualities) their intake of _____ (**C**alories **H**elp **I**ncrease **P**eople's **S**ize) for _____ (**F**reezes **E**very **A**ction...**R**econsider) of being called a _____ _____ (**F**orget **A**ll **T**reats) (**E**at **L**ess **F**ood).

• CHALLENGE
Overcoming roadblocks to appreciating personal value

1. Understanding the potential joys of experiencing longevity:

➢ What would you hope your friends and family would say if they were asked to sum up their feelings about you today? Place a plus (+) next to what they would probably say and a minus (−) next to what they would probably not say.

___self-confident	___conceited	___degrading	___happy	___depressed
___lonely	___positive	___sarcastic	___pleasant	___hostile
___humorous	___self-absorbed	___tired	___passive	___compulsive
___skillful	___angry	___addicted	___smart	___compassionate

___respectful   ___forgiving   ___judgmental   ___enthusiastic   ___trustworthy

___honest   ___reasonable   ___anxious   ___abusive   ___talented

___creative   ___generous   ___responsible   ___organized   ___cooperative

___well-groomed   ___friendly   ___patient   ___open-minded   ___kind

___affectionate   ___rebellious   ___out of shape   ___realistic   ___in shape

___proud   ___attractive   ___stressed   ___valuable   ___thoughtful

___tidy   ___meticulous   ___sloppy   ___overweight   ___slender

___worthwhile   ___successful   ___loving   ___sad   ___secure

___energized   ___flexible   ___caring   ___grumpy   ___useless

___abrasive   ___misunderstood   ___active   ___important   ___happy

___afraid   ___guilt-ridden   ___intimidated   ___resentful   ___jealous

___skeptical   ___bitter   ___cautious   ___bored   ___cruel

___shy   ___enviable   ___loveable   ___emotionally balanced

_____ _____ _____ _____

2. Eliminating fears to allow nurturing of happiness:

➤ What would you hope your friends and family would say if they were asked to describe the negative influences you avoid in your life? Place a check by what you hope they would say you *do not* allow interfering with your life.

___drugs   ___alcohol   ___smoking   ___lack of exercise   ___unhealthy food

___negativity   ___self-pity   ___self-absorption   ___risky behaviors   ___lack of sleep

___overweight   ___underweight   ___sugary drinks   ___inappropriate role models

_____ _____ _____ _____

3. Noticing the signs leading to self-abuse:

➤ Finish the sentence below by underlining any of the listed feelings you might possess that create a detrimental affect on your emotional balance. Place a diagonal line through the words that do not describe your feelings about yourself.

"Most of the time I feel a sense of _____."

depression	anxiety	sleeplessness	anger
irritability	crying	negativity	grief
arguing	loneliness	stress	headaches
fatigue	hostility	distrust	sadness
discontent	withdrawal	rebellion	despair

pain   overachieving   sorrow   remorse

unforgiven   underachievement   oversensitivity   fear

_____   _____   _____   _____

4. Understanding health issues regarding proper nutrition:

The United States is leading the world in the prevalence of overweight and obese citizens. Since 1980 obesity rates have doubled in adults and tripled in adolescents. Nearly one-third of U.S. citizens are obese. Environmental factors in the United States have led to decreased physical activity and increased caloric consumption. In addition, inexpensive foods containing trans fats and high concentrations of sodium have proliferated the fast food industry, prepackaged foods, and prepackaged treats.

Trans fats and sodium (salt) extend shelf life and add flavor to the food. Trans fats are extremely high in calories and fats that contain LDL cholesterol, which is considered "bad cholesterol."

Too much sodium can lead to high blood pressure, cardiovascular diseases, diabetes and kidney disease. We are encouraged to consume low levels of trans fats and sodium and moderate levels of polyunsaturated fats and monounsaturated fats. These fats contain HDL cholesterol, which is considered "good cholesterol."

➤ Place a check by what you believe contributes to the citizens of the United States leading the people of the world in obesity.

____a. Obese people are less active than lean individuals.
____b. Lower food costs due to government subsidies result in inexpensive high-calorie foods.
____c. In 1980 U.S. Government regulations began allowing sweets and fast-food advertising.
____d. All of the above.
____e. All of the above.

____a. People sit at desks at school and work, sit in front of televisions and computers while home.
____b. A majority of children's activities consist of computers, video games, and televisions.
____c. Urban sprawl encourages mechanized transportation rather than walking.
____d. All of the above.
____e. All of the above.

____a. Polyunsaturated fats in moderation are considered good for human health.
____b. Monounsaturated fats in moderation are considered good for human health.
____c. Saturated fats and trans fats should be avoided because they contain "bad cholesterol."
____d. All of the above.
____e. All of the above.

_____a. Trans fats is another name for "partially hydrogenated vegetable oil."

_____b. Trans fats are produced by adding hydrogen to vegetable oil, solidifying the product.

_____c. Trans fats are not easily digestible.

_____d. All of the above.

_____e. All of the above.

_____a. Trans fats are found in margarine.

_____b. Trans fats are found in shortening.

_____c. Trans fats are found in foods to enhance flavor and prolong shelf life.

_____d. All of the above.

_____e. All of the above.

_____a. Trans fats and saturated fats raise the "bad cholesterol" (LDL) in humans.

_____b. A ban on trans fats served in restaurants is spreading throughout the United States.

_____c. Trans fats are a major source of obesity and heart disease in the world.

_____d. All of the above.

_____e. All of the above.

_____a. Too much sodium is not good for human health.

_____b. Trans fats contribute to obesity and poor health.

_____c. Most prepackaged foods contain large quantities of trans fats and sodium.

_____d. All of the above.

_____e. All of the above.

_____a. Food manufacturers in the U.S. are required to list trans fats on the nutrition label.

_____b. Labeling on the front of the package that states "Trans Fats 0" is allowed.

_____c. Labeling on the front of the package that states "Trans Fats 0" can be untrue.

_____d. All of the above.

_____e. All of the above.

_____a. Trans fats and sodium increase the shelf life and taste of food.

_____b. Trans fats and sodium are currently found in the majority of fast foods.

_____c. The fast food industry is beginning to limit the use of trans fats.

_____d. All of the above.

_____e. All of the above.

● Emotional issues affect our desire to eat.

➤ Steve Vaught walked 3,000 miles across the United States in an effort to lose weight. He said, "I thought I had to lose the weight to be happy, but I've discovered you have to be happy to lose the weight."

➤ Is it easiest for you to maintain your proper weight when you are happy?

_____Yes

_____No

- Body size and metabolism rates influence minimum caloric requirements.

➤ Fill in your estimated body weight to determine your estimated daily caloric requirements:

LEVEL OF DAILY ACTIVITY

	SEDENTARY	LOW	MODERATE	STRENUOUS
My body weight in pounds	( )	( )	( )	( )
Calories required per pound	× 10	× 13	× 15	× 18

➤ Calories required per day: _____ _____ _____ _____

- Men are usually larger; consequently, they usually burn more calories that women.

➤ True or False:

_____ Body size, gender, age, and the intensity of activities influence caloric requirements.

- Limit your intake of meat to primarily fish and poultry.

➤ Check the correct answer:

_____a. Beef contains about 2000 calories per pound.
_____b. Chicken contains about 700 calories per pound.
_____c. White fish (halibut, cod, grouper, etc.) contains about 600 calories per pound.
_____d. All of the above.
_____e. All of the above.

- Consume balanced meals with abundant whole grains, fruits, and vegetables.

➤ Check one:

_____a. I feel that I eat the correct amount of healthy food.
_____b. I don't care what I eat or the shape that my body is in.
_____c. I am not certain if I am eating the correct amount of healthy food.
_____d. all of the above.
_____e. none of the above.

- Maintain a regular meal schedule; avoid snacking on prepackaged treats.

➤ Fill in the ideal times of the day for you to consume food:

Breakfast_____ Lunch_____ Dinner_____

- Severely limit your intake of high-calorie fast foods.

  ➢ How many times per month do you partake in meals from fast-food restaurants?
    (check one)

    ____a. Occasionally or never
    ____b. Once or twice a month
    ____c. Three to six times a month
    ____d. Seven to twelve times a month
    ____e. Nearly every day

- Severely limit your intake of sweets and sugary drinks (check one):

    ____a. I am happy with my level of sugar consumption.
    ____b. I would like to reduce my sugar intake.

- Exercise frequently

➢ Fill in the information regarding the activities that you participate in.
  I exercise by (running, weight lifting, yoga, walking, biking, team sports, etc.):

  _____ _____ _____ _____

  _____ _____ _____ _____

  about _____ times per month for a total of about _____ hours per month.

➢ Check one:

    I would like to exercise:

    ____ More
    ____ Less
    ____ The same

- Consider chocolate medicinal; consume only in small amounts.

➢ Check one:

    ____ I do not eat chocolate.
    ____ I consume small amounts of chocolate.
    ____ I am pleased with the balanced amount that I eat.
    ____ I eat too much chocolate.

➤ Below is a list of nourishing foods with sufficient calories for a 150-pound active person for a day of healthy eating. Would this amount of food be sufficient for you? There is abundant information online, including calorie counters, to help you determine your daily caloric requirements. Simply type "calorie counters" into an online search engine.

BREAKFAST	CALORIES
2 medium pancakes/butter/syrup	350
2 oz. ham	110
1/8 honeydew melon	60
6 oz. fruit juice	90
1 cup hot chocolate	150
Breakfast Calories	**760**

LUNCH	CALORIES
2 cups green salad/dressing	100
1 turkey sandwich on wheat bread/mayonnaise	300
8 oz. 2% milk	120
1 apple	100
12 oz. ice tea, sweetened	90
Lunch Calories	**710**

DINNER	CALORIES
4 oz. grilled chicken breast	200
6 oz. baked potato/butter	200
1 cup cooked mixed vegetables	100
8 oz. skim milk	90
1 small muffin	80
1 cup fresh berries	60
12 oz. soda	150
Dinner Calories	**880**

➤ Total calories consumed in a typical day of healthy meals at home:

Breakfast	760
Lunch	710
Dinner	880
Total calories consumed at home	**2,350**

➤ Check the appropriate response:

_____a. I could exist on the amount of food listed above.

_____b. To survive I would require more food.

_____c. I would require less food to survive on a daily basis.

➤ Let's take a look at the calories that can be consumed by eating one day in fast-food restaurants:

FAST FOOD BREAKFAST	CALORIES
Chocolate Cheese Cream Muffin	450
Chocolate Malt Frappuccino Blend	610
Breakfast Calories	**1,060**

FAST FOOD LUNCH	CALORIES
Roasted Chicken Caesar Sandwich	820
Curly Fries	620
Onion Rings	550
Soda	225
Strawberry Banana Ice Cream Shake	1410
Lunch Calories	**3,625**

FAST FOOD DINNER	CALORIES
Whopper Hamburger	726
Large Fries	450
Onion Rings	330
Dutch Apple Pie	308
Cola	225
Dinner Calories	**2,039**

➤ Total calories possibly consumed during a day dining at fast-food restaurants:

Breakfast	1,060
Lunch	3,625
Dinner	2,039
Total calories consumed in fast food restaurants	**6,724**

5. Quantifying the dangers of alcohol, nicotine, and substance abuse:

➤ I would like to (check one):

_____a. Continue not being involved with alcohol, nicotine, or harmful substances.
_____b. Continue my involvement at the current level.
_____c. Reduce my involvement.
_____d. Discontinue my involvement.
_____e. Increase my involvement.

➢ Check the correct answer(s):

     ____a. Alcohol consumption is a problem if it interferes with a person's life.
     ____b. Alcohol consumption is the leading contributor to suicides and homicides.
     ____c. Drinking alcohol can lead to accidents and physical dependency.
     ____d. All of the above.
     ____e. All of the above.

6. Comprehending how hard work can develop self-esteem, dignity, and pride:

Self-worth is a culmination of a person's opinions and feelings stemming from positive or negative beliefs about being worthy, valuable, capable and accepted.

➢ What would you hope your friends and family would say if they were asked to describe their feelings about your capabilities? Check what they would probably say about you.

___valued family member	___role model	___helper	___counselor
___organizer	___teacher	___hard worker	___learner
___athlete	___entertainer	___computer whiz	___listener
___cook	___hiker	___exerciser	___sports fan
___reader	___gamer	___angler	___tourist
___practical joker	___bicyclist	___runner	___investor
___mountaineer	___painter	___supporter	___humorist
___housekeeper	___gift giver	___hobby enthusiast	___provider
___crafter	___handyman	___confidant	___flower grower
___gardener	___historian	___collector	___biker
___conversationalist	___singer	___walker	___investigator
___poet	___inspirer	___seamstress	___movie buff
___gambler	___cleaner	___entrepreneur	___self-starter
___storyteller	___mediator	___hugger	___musician
___friend	___comforter	___preacher	___coach
___card player	___actor	___golfer	___dancer
___smiler	___baby sitter	___shopper	___cheerleader

_____ _____ _____ _____

7. Recognizing signs for the ultimate display of a lack of self-worth:

➢ Refer back to section 3 in this lesson titled "Noticing the signs leading to self-abuse."

How many abusive words did you cross out because they do not describe you? _____

How many abusive words did you underline because they do describe you? _____

➢ Might you possess an imbalance regarding your feelings of self-worth that could potentially lead to self-abuse?

Yes___

No___

• CHANNEL

Attempting to develop pride and dignity while enduring setbacks

1. The joys of longevity:

➤ Many years ago several of our young friends presented their mother with an original handwritten note on mother's day. After the note adorned their refrigerator for many years, Anne shared their message with a church full of mourners celebrating her mother's wonderful life.

Dear Mom

We thank the Lord for you today!
And we thank YOU for:

Enduring the pains of childbirth six times,
For changing thousands upon thousands of diapers,
For wearing the perfume of spit-up year after year,
For putting pretty bows in our hair,
For kissing our boo boos, and praying for us.

For making special birthday cakes,
For helping Santa fill our stockings,
For helping the Easter Bunny hide our baskets,
For wiping our runny noses,
For leaving Valentine treats at our breakfast place.

For doing thousands of loads of laundry,
For cooking us homemade soup and yummy cookies,
For making Halloween costumes,
For letting us have cats and rats and hamsters and fish and dogs,
For putting up with our loud music, and messy rooms, and bad habits.

For being cheerful, even in the most difficult times,
For being there when we needed an ear to listen,
For being unconditionally loving,
For forgiving our mistakes,
For being patient.

For teaching us to say please and thank you,
For giving us freedom to make choices,
For standing by us when they were wrong,
For hugs and kisses . . .
And so much more!

We love you, Mommy

Teresa, Tom, Karen, Anne, David and James

➤ Does this poem encapsulate many of the attributes of being a "loving and lovable person?"

        Yes___

        No___

➤ Is this a realistic example of the compounded joys of living a long life?

        Yes___

        No___

➤ Was there any mention of financial, educational, social, or professional acclaim?

        Yes___

        No___

➤ Would you be honored to receive a similar message from your loved ones?

        Yes___

        No___

➤ Is there someone you would like to honor with a message of your love and appreciation?

        Yes___

        No___

➤ Can you find a piece of paper?

        Yes___

        No___

➤ What would you say about your attributes today? Place a check by the words that best describe you.

___self-confident	___conceited	___degrading	___happy	___depressed
___lonely	___positive	___sarcastic	___pleasant	___hostile
___humorous	___self-absorbed	___tired	___passive	___compulsive
___skillful	___angry	___addicted	___smart	___honest
___compassionate	___respectful	___forgiving	___judgmental	___enthusiastic
___trustworthy	___reasonable	___anxious	___abusive	___talented
___creative	___generous	___responsible	___organized	___cooperative
___well-groomed	___friendly	___patient	___open-minded	___affectionate

___rebellious ___kind ___out of shape ___realistic ___in shape

___proud ___attractive ___stressed ___valuable ___thoughtful

___worthwhile ___successful ___loving ___sad ___secure

___energized ___flexible ___caring ___grumpy ___useless

___abrasive ___misunderstood ___active ___important ___funny

___afraid ___guilt-ridden ___intimidated ___resentful ___jealous

___skeptical ___bitter ___cautious ___bored ___neat

___sloppy ___meticulous ___cruel ___shy ___loveable

___self-starter ___gossiper ___hard worker ___emotionally balanced ___fearful

_____ _____ _____ _____ _____

_____ _____ _____ _____ _____

1. Eliminating fears to allow nurturing of happiness:

➤ What would you say about the negative influences in your life?
Place a check by the things you feel currently interfere with your life.

___drugs ___alcohol ___smoking ___lack of exercise

___improper eating ___negativity ___self-pity ___self-absorption

___risky behaviors ___lack of sleep ___junk food ___fast food

___sweets ___sugary drinks ___lack of goals ___unfair demands from others

___overweight ___carelessness ___recklessness ___inappropriate role models

_____ _____ _____ _____

_____ _____ _____ _____

2. Noticing the signs leading to self-abuse:

➤ Circle the feelings listed below that adversely affect your life. Place a diagonal line through the words that do not describe your feelings.

depression	anxiety	sleeplessness	anger	irritability	crying	negativity
grief	arguing	loneliness	stress	headaches	fatigue	hostility
distrust	sadness	discontent	withdrawal	rebellion	despair	pain
overachieving	sorrow	remorse	unforgiven	underachieving	oversensitive	fear

_____ _____ _____ _____

3. Understanding health issues regarding proper nutrition:

- Emotional issues affect our desire to eat.

➢ Check the following triggers that heighten your desire to eat when and what is not healthy for you:

___celebrating   ___upset   ___depressed   ___anxious   ___nervous

___bored   ___inactive   ___out of shape   ___sad   ___happy

___scared   ___sleepy   ___help sleeping   ___partying   ___tasting

___polite   ___feel better   ___feel satisfied   ___habitual   ___cravings

___tired   ___peer pressure   ___sampling   ___despondence   ___lack of confidence

___fear   ___comfort   ___aroma   ___lack of desire to be physically fit

_____   _____   _____   _____

- Body size and metabolism rates influence minimum caloric requirements.

➢ Check one:

I would like to exercise:

___More

___Less

___The same

Check one:

I am planning to exercise:

___More

___Less

___The same

- Men are usually larger; consequently they usually burn more calories than women. Check the appropriate answer.

_____ a. Men usually burn more calories than women.
_____ b. Men are usually larger than women.
_____ c. More body fat naturally occurs in women than in men.
_____ d. All of the above.
_____ e. All of the above.

- Limit your intake of meat to primarily fish and fowl. Check the answer(s) that indicate your intake of meat products.

_____ a. I eat mostly fish and poultry (fowl).
_____ b. I eat more red meat than fish and fowl.
_____ c. I do not eat meat of any kind.
_____ d. I eat a variety of meats.
_____ e. I eat what's available.

- Consume balanced meals with abundant whole grains, fruits, and vegetables. Indicate your habits for consuming healthy foods. [check the appropriate answer(s)]

    ____ a. I eat mostly white bread and refined flour products.
    ____ b. I eat mostly whole grain cereals and breads.
    ____ c. I usually eat at least five servings of fruits and vegetables per day.

- Maintain a regular meal schedule; avoid snacking on prepackaged treats.

➤ Check the occasions per day that you currently consume food:

   Breakfast____   Brunch____   Lunch____   Snack____   Dinner____   Snack____

➤ Check the occasions per day that would be healthiest for you to consume food:

   Breakfast____   Brunch____   Lunch____   Snack____   Dinner____   Snack____

➤ Limiting or excluding the following treats and drinks will help control my weight:

   ____Cookies   ____Crackers   ____Chips   ____Ice Cream   ____Espresso Drinks

   ____Soda   ____Candy   ____Popcorn   ____Nuts   ____Cake

   ____Rolls   ____Doughnuts   ____Pie   ____Brownies   ____Fruit Snacks

   ____Pudding   ____Pretzels   ____Pastries   ____Biscuits   ____Energy Drinks

   ____Muffins   ____Milk Shakes   ____Dips   ____Energy Bars   ____Hot Chocolate

   _____   _____   _____   _____

- Severely limit your intake of high-calorie fast foods. [check the appropriate answer(s)]

➤ How to avoid high calorie fast foods in your normal diet.

    ____ a. I can usually find more nutritious food at home than in fast-food restaurants.
    ____ b. I am certain that I can consume more meals that are not prepackaged.
    ____ c. I try to take nutritious food from home for meals when I am away from home.
    ____ d. All of the above.
    ____ e. All of the above.

    ____ a. I can read the food nutrition fact labels to avoid eating foods containing trans fats.
    ____ b. I do not need trans fats in my diet to remain healthy.
    ____ c. Trans fats give food longer shelf life while adding cholesterol and calories.
    ____ d. All of the above.
    ____ e. All of the above.

- Severely limit your intake of sweets and sugary drinks.

➤ Let's analyze what will happen if you add just one 12-ounce soda that contains 150 calories to your average daily caloric intake.

TIME PERIOD		APPROXIMATE WEIGHT GAIN
ONE WEEK	$150 \times 7 = 1050$ calories per week	5 ounces
ONE MONTH	$150 \times 30 = 4200$ calories per month	20 ounces
ONE YEAR	$150 \times 365 = 54{,}750$ calories per year	15 pounds
TEN YEARS	15 pounds $\times$ 10 years = 547,750 calories......and _____ pounds gained	

(Fill in, hopefully before you "fill out.")

- Exercise frequently.

➤ Let's look at the calories that are burned by exercising. We have approximated the statistics by describing moderate activity levels involving someone with average weight. Your statistics will differ based on your size, age, gender, level of intensity, and speed of the activities. Select the type of exercise you enjoy being involved in. Do some simple computations to discover the weight control benefits of exercising *one hour daily.* You can determine the benefits of thirty minutes per day by simply dividing all of the numbers in half. Remember; if you are losing any amount of weight...just *any* amount, at least you are not gaining weight!

ACTIVITY	CALORIES PER HOUR	CALORIES PER WEEK	CALORIES PER MONTH	CALORIES PER YEAR	ANNUAL POUNDS SHED
Cooking, playing an instrument, bowling, riding lawn mower	200	1,400	6,083	73,000	20
House work, dancing, fishing, golf, volleyball	300	2,100	9,125	109,500	30
Gardening, horseback riding, mowing lawn	400	2,800	12,166	146,000	40
Aerobics, hiking, race walking, racquetball, skating, skiing, soccer, swimming, tennis, body building	500	3,500	15,208	182,500	51
Bicycling, basketball, football, hockey, rowing	600	4,200	18,250	219,000	61
Rope jumping, running, cross-country skiing	700	4,900	21,233	254,800	70
Handball,	900	6,300	27,375	328,500	91
running from police	1,000	N/A	N/A	N/A	N/A

➢ Select the most appropriate answer:

      ____ a. If I exercise every other day I can divide all of the totals by two.
      ____ b. There is a numerical correlation between the calories burned per hour and weight lost per year.
      ____ c. Exercise is important to develop and help maintain mental health, physical health, and fitness.
      ____ d. All of the above.
      ____ e. All of the above.

      ____ a. The best exercises are the ones that I will do on a consistent basis.
      ____ b. Any exercise is better than none.
      ____ c. It is best to be involved in exercise activities that are enjoyable.
      ____ d. All of the above.
      ____ e. All of the above.

• Consider chocolate medicinal:

➢ A recent Harvard University study discovered that sweets-eaters live about a year longer than those who never touch the stuff. After eating just 1-1/2 ounces of dark chocolate, people showed improved circulation leading to a prolonged life.

➢ Has research suggested that chocolate truly is medicinal?

      Yes ____

      No ____

➢ Are chocolate-covered cherries made by covering cherries with chocolate? Mmmmmmmmmmm!

      Yes ____

4. Quantifying the dangers of alcohol, nicotine, and substance abuse:

➢ The following statistics indicate how consumption of alcohol contributes to death. (Place a check by the answers that you assume are valid.)

      ____ a. 5% of all deaths from diseases of the circulatory system.
      ____ b. 15% of all deaths from diseases of the respiratory system.
      ____ c. 30% of all deaths from accidents caused by fire and flames.
      ____ d. 30% of all accidental drownings.
      ____ e. 30% of all suicides.
      ____ f. 40% of all deaths due to accidental falls.
      ____ g. 45% of all deaths due to automobile accidents.
      ____ h. 60% of all homicides.
      ____ i. All of the above.
      ____ j. All of the above.

➢ Place a check by the correct answer.

      ____ a. Nearly 4% of the U.S. population needs treatment for a diagnosed drug problem.
      ____ b. Nearly 8% of the U.S. population needs treatment for alcohol dependency.
      ____ c. A small percentage of people possessing addictions accept their need for treatment.
      ____ d. All of the above.
      ____ e. All of the above.

_____ a. Drug dependency is defined as needing drugs to overcome discomfort, pain, etc.
_____ b. Drug addiction is using drugs or alcohol regularly despite repeated harmful effects.
_____ c. Physical and psychological withdrawals occur for those who are addicted.
_____ d. All of the above.
_____ e. All of the above.

_____ a. Many people are dependent on prescription drugs that do more good than harm.
_____ b. Using the drugs after the original needs are fulfilled indicates possible addiction.
_____ c. Addiction is apparent if the user's body has a severe reaction upon ceasing usage.
_____ d. All of the above.
_____ e. All of the above.

_____ a. Alcohol and all prescription drugs pose the same risk of addiction.
_____ b. All illicit drugs pose the same risk for addiction.
_____ c. All people are equally susceptible to addiction to drugs and alcohol in exactly the same degree.
_____ d. None of the above.
_____ e. None of the above.

_____ a. There are many proven techniques to overcome drug and alcohol addiction.
_____ b. Techniques for overcoming addiction are medical and psychological in nature.
_____ c. It is wise to seek treatment if drugs or alcohol do more harm than good.
_____ d. All of the above.
_____ e. All of the above.

➤ Nicotine addiction from smoking tobacco is severely impacting the health of people worldwide. Indicate the correct answers with a check mark.

_____ a. Smoking tobacco is the second leading cause of death in the world.
_____ b. Smoking tobacco kills about one in ten people in the world.
_____ c. Studies prove it is easier to overcome heroin addiction than nicotine addition.
_____ d. All of the above.
_____ e. All of the above.

_____ a. Approximately five million annual deaths worldwide are attributed to smoking.
_____ b. Half of the people who smoke will eventually die due to their smoking habit.
_____ c. Ninety-five percent of people who try to stop smoking continue smoking.
_____ d. All of the above.
_____ e. All of the above.

_____ a. Smokers die an average of ten years sooner than nonsmokers.
_____ b. Half of all cancer deaths are attributed to smoking.
_____ c. Most smokers would like to stop smoking.
_____ d. All of the above.
_____ e. All of the above.

_____ a. More people die in the United States per year because of smoking than died in WW II.
_____ b. Expectant mothers harm their babies, and secondhand smoke affects nearly everyone.
_____ c. Smoking kills 157 times more annually in the USA than were lost in the attacks on 9/11.
_____ d. All of the above.
_____ e. All of the above.

_____ a. Smoking-related fires kill untold thousands annually throughout the world.
_____ b. Smoking helps people live a longer, healthier life.
_____ c. Smoking helps breathing become more efficient and creates more lung capacity.
_____ d. All of the above.
_____ e. None of the above.

_____ a. The mother of the author of this book died because of a smoking related illness.
_____ b. Smokers can endanger others because of the secondhand smoke.
_____ c. There are proven methods available to help overcome the smoking habit.
_____ d. All of the above.
_____ e. All of the above.

_____ a. The simplest way to avoid developing the smoking habit is to not begin smoking.
_____ b. The simplest way to avoid developing the smoking habit is to not begin smoking.
_____ c. The simplest way to avoid developing the smoking habit is to not begin smoking.
_____ d. All of the above.
_____ e. All of the above.

➤ Let's take a look at some of the reasons and occasions people smoke cigarettes. Check the triggers that influence people into smoking.

___To be accepted	___Becomes a life style	___Feel more attractive	___Helps self-image
___Stress	___Weight loss	___On a dare	___Acting mature
___Protesting	___Rebellion	___Defiance	___Self-abuse
___Taking a break	___Driving	___Traveling	___After meals
___To belong	___Before sleep	___While partying	___Nervous
___Restless	___Lonely	___Upset	___Bored
___Celebrating	___Happy	___Sad	___Threatened
___Coerced	___Feeling cool	___Identity	___Pass the time
___Out of habit	___To seem intelligent	___Feeling sophisticated	___Hooked on advertising
___Displaying independence		___Immediately upon waking	
___While drinking alcohol		___Influence of role models	

_____   _____   _____   _____

_____   _____   _____   _____

➤ Check the following words that can effectively finish this statement. "If I quit smoking, or better yet never start, I will more likely avoid:

___Smelling like smoke	___Stained teeth	___Cancer
___Emphysema	___Wrinkled skin	___Uncontrollable cravings
___Bad breath	___Losing sense of smell	___Heart disease
___Sore throat	___Coughing	___Harming others
___900 hours annually wasted	___Finger stains	___Littering
___Accidental fires	___Being excluded	___Throat phlegm
___Losing energy	___Many illnesses	___Early death
___Being a bad role model	___Feeling ashamed	___Feeling lack of control
___Needing to carry cigarettes	___Shortness of breath	___Withdrawals
___Wasting thousands of dollars	___Being controlled by nicotine	

_____   _____   _____   _____

➤ Check the following answers that can effectively complete this statement: "If I smoke or would ever begin smoking, the things that would probably help me stop smoking would be:

___Setting a date to quit

___Informing friends of my plans to quit

___Asking my friends for support

___Keeping my plans to quit a secret

___Replacing cigarettes with gum, candy, exercise, etc.

___Staying away from occasions of temptation

___Carrying a favorite photo or souvenir in place of the cigarette pack

___Breathing deeply through my nose

___Sitting in no-smoking sections

___Discarding all of my cigarettes, lighters, ashtrays, matches, etc.

___Writing down my feelings about quitting in a diary

___Chatting with nonsmokers online and in person

___Making a list of people who don't want me to die

___Carrying photos of people who would miss me if I die

___Seeking help from my doctor

___Spending time with nonsmokers

___Asking friends and family to write me notes of why they think I should quit

___Seeking new environments and activities that discourage or forbid smoking

___Visiting with patients in a hospital pulmonary ward

___Imagining I am a patient in one of the beds in the pulmonary ward

___Carrying a photograph of myself before I smoked

___Visiting with successful quitters and hearing their success stories

___Listing acquaintances who have died due to nicotine addiction

___Informing loved ones that I am giving them a special gift…a smokeless me

___Rewarding myself with a variety of activities, hobbies, vacations, etc.

___Listing the reasons why I would like to live ten years longer

___Listing the physical activities I could engage in more successfully

___Listing what I would buy if I wasn't spending money on cigarettes

___Listing where people smoke outside because smoking is not allowed inside

___Quitting in memory of those I have known who have been my reverse role models

___Living in the NOW (**N**ever **O**verlook **W**ishes)

_____

_____

_____

_____

5. Comprehending how hard work can develop self-esteem, dignity and pride:

➢ Explain something that you have accomplished that has given you a feeling of self-esteem, dignity, and pride. It may have been a hobby, something at school, volunteering, working, sports, family related, etc.

_____

_____

_____

_____

_____

_____

154

6. Recognizing signs for the ultimate display of a lack of self-worth:

➤ Write in True or False (CLUE: all answers are the same).

_____Traffic accidents are the leading cause of injurious deaths in the world.

_____Suicides are the second leading cause of injurious deaths in the world.

_____Homicides are the third leading cause of injurious deaths in the world.

_____Suicides and homicides combined cause more deaths per year than traffic accidents.

_____Humans deliberately kill themselves and others more than all traffic deaths combined.

_____The person who will most likely deliberately kill you is currently wearing your clothing.

➤ Suicide is an anxious cry for help. If you feel suicidal or know someone who does, please seek professional help to escape from the downward spiral of self-abuse.

True or False

_____Suicide should be the most preventable of all injurious deaths.

_____Statistics indicate that suicide is the most preventable manner of exiting this earth.

• CHECK

"Success is peace of mind which is a direct result of satisfaction in knowing you did your best to become the best you are capable of becoming." —John Wooden

➤ On a scale from 0 to 10, 10 being high, select and insert the numbers depicting the level of your feelings regarding the balance in your life. Add the numbers and transfer the total to develop the graph following the three assessment forms. Hopefully this will assist you in ascertaining the balance of your purpose, pleasure, and peace of mind.

PURPOSE

Work...School...Responsibilities

0	1	2	3	4	5	6	7	8	9	10

Confused/Lacking Vision _____ Clear Mission

Bored/Burnt Out _____ Challenged/Enthused

Pressured/Negative _____ Praised/Positive

Fearful/Anxious _____ Safe/Secure

Incapable/Unteachable _____ Competent/Skilled

Lazy/Lethargic _____ Productive/Improved

Rejected/Undeserving _____ Needed/Worthy

Disloyal/Slow _____ Committed/Hard Worker

Uncooperative _____ Supportive

Disgusting/Selfish _____ Loving/Sharing

TOTAL _____

PLEASURE

Activities...Hobbies...Leisure Time

0	1	2	3	4	5	6	7	8	9	10

Anguish/Apathetic	_____	Enjoyable/Interested
Drained/Fatigued	_____	Renewed/Rested
Tense/Demands	_____	Relaxed/Contributor
Frustrated/Punished	_____	Fulfilled/Rewarded
Insufficient Time	_____	Enough Time
Clock Slows Down	_____	Clock Speeds Up
Enemies/Lonely	_____	Close Friends/Pets
Stymied/Stuck	_____	Inspired/Motivated
Drudgery/Dull	_____	Fun/Excited
Restricted	_____	Freedom
TOTAL	_____	

PEACE OF MIND

Personal...Family...Home

0	1	2	3	4	5	6	7	8	9	10

Ignored/Belittled	_____	Valued/Appreciated
Depressed/Angry	_____	Happy/Contented
Malnourished/Sleepy	_____	Nourished/Rested
Self-Absorbed/Greedy	_____	Generous/Sharing
Harassed/Abused	_____	Respected/Treasured
Guilt-Ridden/Petrified	_____	Forgiven/Resilient
Isolated/Excuses	_____	Belong/Responsible
Liar/Deceitful	_____	Honest/Trusting
Procrastinator/Broke	_____	Organized/Funded
Repulsive/Unpleasant	_____	Loveable/Enjoyable
TOTAL	_____	

➢ Transfer the three numerical totals you computed on the three previous forms.

Shade in the appropriate blanks from left to right to develop a graph signifying how you are currently balancing your Purpose, Pleasure, and Peace of Mind.

NUMERICAL TOTALS

DEVELOP A GRAPH USING THE TOTALS ON LEFT

_____ PURPOSE

_____ PLEASURE

_____ PEACE OF MIND

0   10   20   30   40   50   60   70   80   90   100

➢ After analyzing the results I feel I need to spend more time and effort:

_____

_____

_____

_____

➢ After analyzing the results I feel I need to spend less time and effort:

_____

_____

_____

_____

• **CONFIDENCE**

Self-worth is a product of balancing purpose, pleasure, and peace of mind.

➤ List a primary goal and possibly a secondary goal on the following forms to help establish and track your visions of enhancing your self-worth.

ASSESSING GOALS*

List your goal(s) and assign a number from 0 to 10 (10 being high) to each consideration of the goals setting process.

GOALS ➤➤➤➤➤➤➤➤➤ _____   _____
                                                (Primary Goal)   (Secondary Goal)

	(Primary Goal)	(Secondary Goal)
1. Level of need/passion	_____	_____
2. Level of desire to sacrifice	_____	_____
3. Level of research/planning	_____	_____
4. Level of action/skills	_____	_____
5. Ability to accept change	_____	_____
6. Ability to endure criticism	_____	_____
7. Available resources/assistance	_____	_____
8. Available time/energy	_____	_____
9. History of patience	_____	_____
10. History of commitment	_____	_____

Probability Index Total   _____   _____

Probability Index Scoring

90–100 . . . . . . Celebrate!	40–49 . . . . . . Should you reassess your goal?
80–89 . . . . Go for it!	30–39 . . . . . . Was your addition correct?
70–79 . . . . Have you analyzed obstacles?	20–29 . . . . . . Did you follow the directions?
60–69 . . . . Can you change anything?	10–19 . . . . . . Is it time for a reality check?
50–59 . . . . Is it worth the risk?	0–9 . . . . . . Possibly seek professional help?

*Greatness Only Awaits Labor…Staaaaaaaaaart!

_____

(CHAPTER TITLE)

_____

(GOAL/VISION/DREAM)

There is a need because:

_____

_____

The change, sacrifices and criticism that need to be addressed are:

_____

_____

_____

The assistance and resources that need to be procured are:

_____

_____

The history of patience and commitment has been:

_____

_____

In order to reach the goal I will:

_____

_____

_____

_____

_____

_____

_____

The beginning timeline is:

Set Goals	Planning	Implement	Completion?	Completed!
___/___/_____	___/___/_____	___/___/_____	___/___/_____	___/___/_____

The celebration plans are:

_____

_____

_____

(CHAPTER TITLE)

_____

(GOAL/VISION/DREAM)

There is a need because:

_____

_____

The change, sacrifices and criticism that need to be addressed are:

_____

_____

_____

The assistance and resources that need to be procured are:

_____

_____

The history of patience and commitment has been:

_____

_____

In order to reach the goal I will:

_____

_____

_____

_____

_____

_____

The beginning timeline is:

Set Goals	Planning	Implement	Completion?	Completed!
___/___/____	___/___/____	___/___/____	___/___/____	___/___/____

The celebration plans are:

_____

_____

Indicate the acronyms that will help you achieve your goals.

ABUSE	All Beings Underestimate Some Eventualities
AMENDS	Always Manage Every Negative Discussion/Sorry
ATTITUDE	All Terrific Thoughts Incorporate True Unrelenting Dedication to Excellence
BELIEVE	Bountiful Experiences Loved If Everyone Visualizes Eventualities
BUSY	Bosses Usually Stress You
CHEATED	Circumventing Honest Efforts Alienates Trust Every Day
CHIPS	Calories Help Increase People's Size
CHOIR	Caring Hearts Offer Inspired Relationships
CONFIDENCE	Changing Our Negative Fears Invites Delightful Experiences Never Considered Easy
COOPERATE	Change Offers Opportunities People Eventually Realize And Teamwork Excels
COST	Concentrating Only Saves Time
DESIRE	Does Everyone Strive In Reaching Excellence
DIGNITY	Depicting Integrity Granting Nobility In Thy Years
DOPE	Does Overuse Paralyze Empowerment
DOPER	Does Overuse Produce Extinguishing Results
DRUGS	Do Results Ultimately Guarantee Success
FACT	Finding Actual Circumstances True
FAT	Forget All Treats
FAT ELF	Forget All Treats, Eat Less Food
FEAR	Find Each Anxiety'n Repair
FEAR	Freezes Every Action; Reconsider
FUN	Forget Unnecessary Nonsense
GOALS	Greatness Only Awaits Labor . . . Staaaaaart
GUN	Give Up Now
HABITS	How All Beings Imprint Traits
HARD WORK	Happiness Awaits Relentless Desire; We Only Respect Kindness
HEART	Help Everyone Achieve Respect Today
HIGH	Help Individuals Get Happy
HONOR	Helping Others Needing Our Respect
HOPE	Harnessing Optimism Produces Empowerment
IDEA	Inspiration Deserves Everyone's Attention
IMPROVE	Individuals Make Progress Rewarding Our Valiant Efforts
JOYS	Just Offer Your Spirit
MUSIC	Mankind's Ultimate Study In Creation
NERVES	Negative Energy Ruins Visions; Envision Success
PAIN	People Always Inherit Nerves
PEACE	Practicing Effective Attitudes Calms Everyone
PERFECT	Pursuing Everything Right, Forgetting Every Care Tactfully
PRIDE	People Respect Individuals Delivering Excellence
REWARD	Realizing Everyone's Work Assures Recognition Deserved

RIGHT	Respecting Integrity Grants Honor Today
TALENT	To Achieve, Latent Energy Needs Training
TEAMWORK	Tolerance Empowers All Members; We Only Respect Kindness
TRAGEDY	Terrible Results Accentuate Grief; Everyone Deliriously Yearns
TRUE	To Rely Upon Everything
WORK	We Only Respect Kindness

SELF-WORTH

www.CharacterConstructionCompany.com

ACROSS

1 Forget All Treats
3 Practicing Effective Attitudes Calms Everyone
6 Circumventing Honest Efforts Alienates Trust Every Day
8 People Always Inherit Nerves
9 Depicting Nobility Granting Nobility In Thy Years
10 Just Offer Your Spirit
12 Concentrating Only Saves Time
13 Pursuing Everything Right, Forgetting Every Care Tactfully
15 Find Each Anxiety'n Repair
16 We Only Respect Kindness
18 To Rely Upon Everything
23 Inspiration Deserves Everyone's Attention
25 Give Up Now
26 Individuals Make Progress Rewarding Our Valiant Efforts
27 To Achieve; Latent Energy Needs Training
28 Helping Others Needing Our Respect
30 Does Overuse Produce Extinguishing Results
32 Forget All Treats Eat Less Food
34 All Beings Underestimate Some Eventualities
35 Do Results Ultimately Guarantee Success
38 Change Offers Opportunities People Eventually Realize And Teamwork Excels
39 Bosses Usually Stress You
40 Bountiful Experiences Loved If Everyone Visualizes Eventualities

DOWN

2 All Terrific Thoughts Incorporate True Unrelenting Dedication to Excellence
4 Calories Help Increase People's Size
5 Happiness Awaits Relentless Desire We Only Respect Kindness
6 Changing Our Negative Fears Invites Delightful Experiences Never Considered Easy
7 Does Overuse Paralyze Empowerment
11 Help Everyone Achieve Respect Today
14 Mankinds Ultimate Study In Creation
15 Forget Unnecessary Nonsense
17 Realizing Everyone's Work Assures Recognition Deserved
19 Respecting Integrity Grants Honor Today
20 Caring Hearts Offer Inspired Relationships
21 Negative Energy Ruins Visions; Envision Success
22 Harnessing Optimism Produces Empowerment
24 Always Manage Every Negative Discussion Sorry
27 Tolerance Empowers All Members; We Only Respect Kindness
28 How All Beings Imprint Traits
29 Terrible Results Accentuate Grief Everyone Deliriously Yearns
30 Does Everyone Strive In Reaching Excellence
31 Help Individuals Get Happy
33 Find All Circumstances True
36 Greatness Only Awaits Labor Start
37 People Respect Individuals Delivering Excellence

SELF-WORTH

Find the words in the grid. When you are done, the unused letters in the grid will spell out a hidden message. Pick them out from left to right, top line to bottom line. Words can go horizontally, vertically and diagonally in all eight directions.

```
F O R E P O D R F A T E L F G E T A L
L N U G T P E A C E H R E A S P I H C
T S C O S T E A C T B O L E S S M F O
E K H O D H I G H I T E N D R B P Y S
C R O K B D Y F N A S B L O W U R T E
N O P K E Y D U F X P U H I R S O D V
E W E A E N E N N M L F M G E Y V M R
D D D G S H A T T I T U D E V E W E
I R T Y U H A T D D K R O W M A E T N
F A V N B N R N R I X H X R G L P K P
N H N L A A T E A G L H F O B E E N M
O S B D E J C L W N Z W A E T P R C L
C Y G H E H T A E I R L V A A S F T M
H S B U E S D T R T S P R R D R E C X
N C T A R O I R F Y M E R N I K C A N
R E T I P D I R K L P N E I Y O T F M
H E U E B G J R E O I M T Q D K H H P
D K B R H A O W O A A J J Q R E X C D
L H X T T W H C P Y S Y O J B J X P V
```

www.CharacterConstructionCompany.com

ABUSE	COOPERATE	FATELF	HONOR	PERFECT
AMENDS	COST	FEAR	HOPE	PRIDE
ATTITUDE	DESIRE	FUN	IDEA	REWARD
BELIEVE	DIGNITY	GOALS	IMPROVE	RIGHT
BUSY	DOPE	GUN	JOYS	TALENT
CHEATED	DOPER	HABITS	MUSIC	TEAMWORK
CHIPS	DRUGS	HARDWORK	NERVES	TRAGEDY
CHOIR	FACT	HEART	PAIN	TRUE
CONFIDENCE	FAT	HIGH	PEACE	WORK

TEAMWORK
Tolerance Empowers All Members;
Wisdom Offers Renewed Kindness

• CONNECT

A team is two or more people interacting together

Deciding whether to _____ (**F**erocious **I**nsults **G**uarantee **H**igh **T**ensions), flee, or

flow helps the _____ (**T**olerance **E**mpowers **A**ll **M**embers) learn to _____

(**W**isdom **O**ffers **R**enewed **K**indness) together. People who are _____ (**L**osers **A**lways **Z**ap **Y**a)

and possess inflated _____ (**E**verybody **G**ags **O**n **S**elfishness) cause members to

_____ (**A**lways **R**epeating **G**arbage **U**nnerves **E**veryone) and get _____

(**M**eanness **A**lways **D**estroys), acting like _____ (**I**ndividual's **D**ebilitating **I**deas **O**ffend **T**eams)

rather than trying to _____ (**H**urry, **E**veryone **L**oves **P**rogress) the other team members

achieve _____ (**S**eek **U**nderstanding **C**arefully; **C**haracter **E**ventually **S**ows **S**atisfaction).

• CHALLENGE

"I don't want to just win the game; I want to win the guy."—Eddie Robinson

1. Learning team expectations:

➤ Imagine you are responsible for selecting a team of people, either at home, work or play.
   Place a plus sign (+) by the words that would best finish the following sentence.
   Place a minus sign (−) by the words that you feel would be inappropriate.

   "If I were selecting a team I would want everyone to be _____."

__selfish	__courteous	__whiners	__negative	__jealous
__proud	__egotistical	__nice	__gracious	__vibrant
__patient	__polite	__respectful	__self-centered	__caring
__goal-oriented	__argumentative	__helpful	__angry	__lazy
__humorous	__complainers	__empowered	__threatened	__fair
__gossipers	__helpers	__quitters	__humble	__responsible

__positive	__inspirational	__learners	__liars	__empathetic
__confident	__disciplined	__ethical	__hateful	__hopeful
__loyal	__trustworthy	__happy	__hard workers	__tolerant
__winners	__fast	__healthy	__blamers	__committed
__witty	__smiling	__organized	__cooperative	__on time
__reliable	__optimistic	__visionaries	__curious	__wise
__upset	__jerks	__slow	__confrontational	__leaders
__understanding	__decisive	__self-absorbed	__hypocritical	__judgmental
__smart	__late	__mean	__analytical	__motivated
__creative	__sour	__involved	__sad	__honest
__full of excuses	__bluffers	__sincere	__heroes	__trained
__enjoyable	__mad	__sweet	__isolated	__sarcastic
__intimidating	__harassing	__satisfied	__appreciated	__slow
__procrastinators	__back stabbers	__successful	__braggers	__thorough
__grateful	__abrasive	__planners	__energized	__safe
__inconsistent	__unified	__rude	__greedy	__giving
__bullies	__quality conscious	__intelligent	__contributors	__risk takers
__thinkers	__fun	__talented	__educated	__careful
__complimentary	__driven	__tunnel-visionaries	__appreciative	__shy
__sharing	__communicative	__productive	__friendly	__teachable
__attentive	__coachable	__competitive	__vindictive	__pliable
__resourceful	__mediocre	__honest	__skillful	__patient
__forgiving	__abusive	__dedicated	__losers	__credible
__achievers	__planners	__self-starters	__enthusiastic	__idiots
__compassionate	__trainable	__sensitive	__experienced	__clean
__knowledgeable	__persevering	__confiding	__believable	__brave
__encouraging	__valuable	__supportive	__interested	__assertive
__tubular-visionaries	__volatile	__balanced	__stable	__tenacious
__dependable	__flexible	__resilient	__proactive	__listeners
__entertainers	__apathetic	__passive	__uninvolved	__secure
__desirous	__accusers	__bossy	__manipulative	__consistent
__opportunistic	__ambitious	__accomplishers	__selfless	__rested
__perfectionists	__indecisive	__self-indulged	__conceited	__unrealistic
__forceful	__joyous	__accomplished	__jackasses	__loving
__bright	__kind	_____	_____	_____
_____	_____			

➤ There are many effective methods of complimenting others to recognize the positive attributes on the preceding listing. Let's look at some ways of sharing complimentary affirmations in group settings.

➤ Ask eight or more people who have known one another for a period of time to be seated in a circle. Provide each participant with a sheet of paper and a similar pen or pencil. Ask everyone to print their name on the top of their paper. Instruct the team to pass their paper to the person on their immediate right. Ask everyone to write three short affirmations scattered throughout the paper. When everyone is finished writing three positive statements pass the papers to the right. Continue the process until the documents arrive at the person to the left of the originator of the page. That person will read the compliments aloud to the group and then ceremoniously present the originator with the list of affirmations.

➤ Place one "affirmer's chair" in front of a group or in the center of a circle of people who have known one another for a period of time. Individuals have the opportunity to be seated in the special chair when they feel the desire to express their feelings to others. Only the person in the "affirmer's chair" is allowed to speak; it is imperative that everyone else remain silent. Assign a person to enforce the "no talking guideline" and potentially establish a time limit. Invite participants to individually address the group from the "affirmer's chair." The person in the "affirmer's chair" has the opportunity to say things like "Bubba, I'm sorry I made you so upset about... Karen, I absolutely love the way you play the harp; I'm sure the angels will greet you with open arms! Carl, congratulations on becoming an Eagle Scout; you have been such an inspiration and magnificent role model for all of us. Joey, you always have a huge smile on your face; you are such a positive and loving guy, I want to be just like you!"

➤ Everyone in the group can tape, staple, or glue a piece of paper to a heavy piece of construction paper, cardboard, etc. Participants help one another affix the "customized notepads" to each other's backs. They can be taped, pinned, hung with twine, etc. The group can be organized in circles or lines. The process can begin with everyone facing the same direction while holding a pen or pencil with a notepad attached to their back. Everyone can write a personal note on the person's back directly in front of them. You might want to establish a time limit or limit the number of words. Ask all of the people to turn around at the same time and repeat the process. Then shift the entire line or suggest everyone move to the person they know the least or possibly the best. This is an opportunity for individuals to offer an apology, congratulations, an encouragement, a thank you, a remembrance, etc. To conclude the event, divide everyone in pairs. Each duo can exchange notes and read them aloud or simply to one another. Remember to set time or word limits.

2. Deciding when to fight, flee, or flow:

➤ Insert words from the previous listing that could potentially incite a verbal or physical "fight."

_____   _____   _____   _____

_____   _____   _____   _____

➤ Insert words from the "team expectations listing" that can influence your decision regarding possibly leaving, or "fleeing," a group or team.

_____   _____   _____   _____

_____   _____   _____   _____

➤ Insert words from the "team expectations listing" that make "flowing" with a group or team more enjoyable.

_____   _____   _____   _____

_____   _____   _____   _____

3. Understanding how to avoid arguments:

➤ Dale Carnegie says: "The only way to win an argument is to

[circle one]   not argue   argue."

➤ An ancient Chinese proverb states: "He who strikes the first blow admits he

[circle one]   won the argument   lost the argument."

➤ Insert significant words from the "team expectations listing" that you feel help initiate arguments.

_____   _____   _____   _____

_____   _____   _____   _____

_____   _____   _____   _____

4. Learning to employ the six steps of conflict resolution:

➤ Check the steps that you feel are important in resolving conflicts.

_____Select your battle; know the resolution you would like to attain.
_____Avoid attacking individuals; focus on the facts.
_____Discuss the possible resolutions as soon as possible at the lowest level.
_____Proceed through the appropriate chain of command.
_____Determine when to end your pursuit and/or when to seek assistance.
_____Continually analyze if the emotional energy expended justifies the desired outcome?

5. Quantifying the five steps of the flow formula:

➤ Fill in the numbers to place the five steps of the flow formula in order.

_____Feed the flow.
_____Fire up the flow.
_____Freeze the flow.
_____Fix the flow.
_____Follow the flow.

• CHANNEL

"Individual commitment to a group effort—that is what makes a team work, a company work, a society work, a civilization work." —Vince Lombardi

1. Learning team expectations:

➤ Describe how you respond as a member of a team, either at home, work or play. Place a plus sign (+) by the words that would best finish the following sentence. Place a minus sign (−) by the words that you feel would be inappropriate.

"When I am a member of a team I am _____."

__selfish	__courteous	__a whiner	__negative	__jealous
__proud	__egotistical	__nice	__gracious	__vibrant
__patient	__polite	__respectful	__self-centered	__caring
__goal-orientated	__argumentative	__helpful	__angry	__lazy
__humorous	__a complainer	__empowered	__a threatener	__fair
__a gossiper	__a helper	__a quitter	__humble	__responsible
__positive	__inspirational	__a learner	__a liar	__empathetic
__confident	__disciplined	__ethical	__hateful	__hopeful
__loyal	__trustworthy	__happy	__a hard worker	__tolerant
__a winner	__successful	__healthy	__a blamer	__committed
__witty	__a smiler	__organized	__cooperative	__on time
__reliable	__optimistic	__a visionary	__curious	__wise
__upset	__a jerk	__mediocre	__confrontational	__a leader
__understanding	__decisive	__self-absorbed	__hypocritical	__judgmental
__smart	__late	__mean	__analytical	__motivated
__creative	__sour	__involved	__sad	__honest
__full of excuses	__a bluffer	__sincere	__a hero	__trained
__enjoyable	__mad	__sweet	__isolated	__sarcastic
__intimidating	__harassing	__satisfied	__appreciated	__loving
__a procrastinator	__a back stabber	__successful	__a bragger	__thorough
__grateful	__abrasive	__a planner	__energized	__safe
__inconsistent	__unifying	__rude	__greedy	__giving
__a bully	__quality conscious	__intelligent	__a contributor	__a risk taker
__a thinker	__fun	__talented	__educated	__careful
__complimentary	__driven	__tunnel-visionary	__appreciative	__shy
__sharing	__communicative	__productive	__friendly	__teachable
__attentive	__coachable	__competitive	__vindictive	__pliable
__resourceful	__messy	__honest	__skillful	__patient

___forgiving   ___abusive   ___dedicated   ___a loser   ___credible

___an achiever   ___a planner   ___a self-starter   ___enthusiastic   ___an idiot

___compassionate   ___trainable   ___sensitive   ___experienced   ___clean

___knowledgeable   ___persevering   ___confiding   ___believable   ___brave

___encouraging   ___valuable   ___supportive   ___interested   ___assertive

___a tubular-visionary   ___volatile   ___balanced   ___stable   ___tenacious

___dependable   ___flexible   ___resilient   ___proactive   ___a listener

___an entertainer   ___apathetic   ___passive   ___uninvolved   ___secure

___desirous   ___an accuser   ___bossy   ___manipulative   ___consistent

___opportunistic   ___ambitious   ___an accomplisher   ___selfless   ___rested

___a perfectionist   ___indecisive   ___self-indulged   ___conceited   ___unrealistic

___forceful   ___joyous   ___accomplished   ___jackass   ___slow

___bright   ___kind

_____   _____   _____   _____   _____

➤ List several descriptive words for productive team expectations and for expectations that will probably be unproductive.

PRODUCTIVE TEAM EXPECTATIONS	**UNPRODUCTIVE TEAM EXPECTATIONS**
_____	_____
_____	_____
_____	_____
_____	_____
_____	_____
_____	_____

2. Deciding when to fight, flee, or flow:

➢ Finish the following statements.

"I decided to fight in a situation when . . .

_____

_____

_____

"I decided to flee from a situation when . . .

_____

_____

_____

"I decided to flow with a situation because . . .

_____

_____

_____

3. Understanding how to avoid arguments:

➢ Describe what will potentially launch you into an argumentative mode and explain how you can best avoid that situation.

_____

_____

_____

_____

➢ Fill in the blanks describing how you can potentially apologize for something you might say or do to offend someone.

"I am sorry and I apologize because I now understand that I offended you when I said (did)_____

_____

I said (did) it because I was _____

I was wrong and I should have said (done) _____

In the future I am planning to_____

so that doesn't happen again. I sincerely hope you accept my apology because I value our

relationship more than_____."

4. Learning to employ the six steps of conflict resolution:

➤ Describe how you have pursued (or wish you would have pursued) the following steps dealing
   with a conflict you have encountered or a conflict that you have imagined.

What was the battle you selected and the resolution you hoped to attain?

_____

_____

_____

How did you avoid attacking individuals and focus on the facts?

_____

_____

_____

At which level did you begin discussing the options?

_____

_____

_____

What would you change in the way you followed the appropriate chain of command?

_____

_____

_____

When and why did you end your pursuit or did you ask for assistance? Did you attain your desired
outcome?

_____

_____

_____

➤ Was the outcome worth your emotional energy?

On a scale from 1 to 10 (10 being high) circle the level of emotional energy you expended?

1   2   3   4   5   6   7   8   9   10

5. Quantifying the five steps of the flow formula:

➤ Relate a situation you have experienced that exemplifies the five steps of the flow formula.

During a group discussion _____ (person's name or initials) "fired up the flow"

by providing a plan of action regarding _____ and [list name(s)]

_____, _____, _____ "fed

the flow" with ideas and suggestions. Then most of the remainder of the group (list name[s])

_____, _____, _____,

_____ jumped on board and "followed the flow." However,

_____ (name) questioned the proceedings and consequently "froze the

flow." Finally _____ (name) offered a remedy that "fixed the flow" leading

to a successful resolution.

• CHECK

"Coming together is a beginning.
Keeping together is progress.
Working together is success." —Henry Ford

➤ "I feel I can become a better team member if I . . .

_____

_____

_____

• CONFIDENCE

A successful team beats with one heart.

➤ List one or two goals on the following forms that will help you strengthen your teams.

176

ASSESSING GOALS*

List your goal(s) and assign a number from 0 to 10 (10 being high) to each consideration of the goals setting process.

GOALS ➤➤➤➤➤➤➤➤➤ _____   _____
                                            (Primary Goal)   (Secondary Goal)

	(Primary Goal)	(Secondary Goal)
1. Level of need/passion	_____	_____
2. Level of desire to sacrifice	_____	_____
3. Level of research/planning	_____	_____
4. Level of action/skills	_____	_____
5. Ability to accept change	_____	_____
6. Ability to endure criticism	_____	_____
7. Available resources/assistance	_____	_____
8. Available time/energy	_____	_____
9. History of patience	_____	_____
10. History of commitment	_____	_____

Probability Index Total   _____   _____

Probability Index Scoring

90–100 . . . . . . Celebrate!
80–89 . . . . Go for it!
70–79 . . . . Have you analyzed obstacles?
60–69 . . . . Can you change anything?
50–59 . . . . Is it worth the risk?

40–49 . . . . . . Should you reassess your goal?
30–39 . . . . . . Was your addition correct?
20–29 . . . . . . Did you follow the directions?
10–19 . . . . . . Is it time for a reality check?
0–9 . . . . . . Possibly seek professional help?

*Greatness Only Awaits Labor…Staaaaaaaaaart!

_____

(CHAPTER TITLE)

_____

(GOAL/VISION/DREAM)

There is a need because:

_____

_____

The change, sacrifices and criticism that need to be addressed are:

_____

_____

_____

The assistance and resources that need to be procured are:

_____

_____

The history of patience and commitment has been:

_____

_____

In order to reach the goal I will:

_____

_____

_____

_____

_____

_____

_____

The beginning timeline is:

Set Goals	Planning	Implement	Completion?	Completed!
___/___/____	___/___/____	___/___/____	___/___/____	___/___/____

The celebration plans are:

_____

_____

_____

(CHAPTER TITLE)

_____

(GOAL/VISION/DREAM)

There is a need because:

_____

_____

The change, sacrifices and criticism that need to be addressed are:

_____

_____

_____

The assistance and resources that need to be procured are:

_____

_____

The history of patience and commitment has been:

_____

_____

In order to reach the goal I will:

_____

_____

_____

_____

_____

_____

_____

The beginning timeline is:

Set Goals	Planning	Implement	Completion?	Completed!
___/___/_____	___/___/_____	___/___/_____	___/___/_____	___/___/_____

The celebration plans are:

_____

_____

Indicate the acronyms that will help you achieve your goals.

ARGUE	Always Repeating Garbage Unnerves Everyone
EGOS	Everybody Gags On Selfishness
FEEL	Fear Eventually Eliminates Love
FIGHT	Ferocious Insults Generate High Tensions
HELP	Hurry Everyone Loves Progress
IDEA	Inspiration Deserves Everyone's Attention
IDIOTS	Individual's Debilitating Ideas Offend Team
JOYS	Just Open Your Soul
LAZY	Losers Always Zap Ya
MAD	Meanness Always Destroys
OOPS	Opportunities Often Pass Swiftly
PROGRESS	People Reform Or Garner Refinement, Establishing Some Success
TRY	To Respect Yourself
WORK	We Only Respect Kindness

TEAMWORK

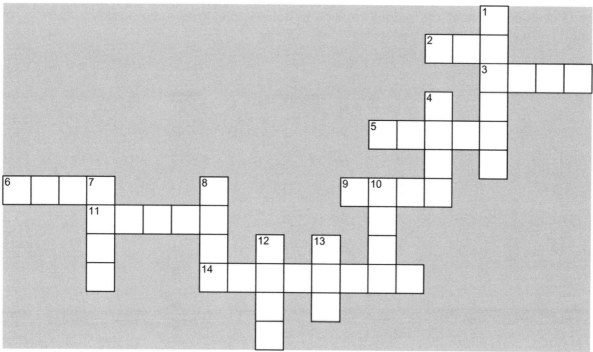

www.CharacterConstructionCompany.com

ACROSS

2 Meanness Always Destroys
3 Inspiration Deserves Everyone's Attention
5 Ferocious Insults Generate High Tensions
6 Fear Eventually Eliminates Love
9 Just Open Your Soul
11 Always Repeating Garbage Unnerves Everyone
14 People Reform Or Garner Refinement Establishing Some Success

DOWN

1 Individual's Debilitating Ideas Offends Teams
4 Everybody Gags On Selfishness
7 Losers Always Zap Ya
8 Hurry Everyone Loves Progress
10 Opportunities Often Pass Swiftly
12 We Only Respect Kindness
13 To Respect Yourself

TEAMWORK

Find the words in the grid. When you are done, the unused letters in the grid will spell out a hidden message. Pick them out from left to right, top line to bottom line. Words can go horizontally, vertically and diagonally in all eight directions.

```
T  T  O  L  E  R  A  L  I  N
W  R  S  Y  O  J  E  D  C  E
O  Y  Y  E  M  E  I  I  P  O
R  D  Z  W  F  O  H  D  E  R
K  A  S  A  T  A  S  E  L  L
M  M  E  S  L  M  O  A  L  S
B  E  R  S  F  H  G  K  P  P
F  I  G  H  T  B  E  O  R  M
D  M  D  K  D  M  O  L  D  Z
W  P  R  O  G  R  E  S  S  L
```

www.CharacterConstructionCompany.com

EGOS	LAZY
FEEL	MAD
FIGHT	OOPS
HELP	PROGRESS
IDEA	TRY
IDIOTS	WORK
JOYS	

INTEGRITY
Individuals Never Trust Evil;
Golden Rule Inspires Their Years

- ## CONNECT

Is your word good; are you known for your honesty; can you be trusted?

A person who is in a leadership position can be a _____ (**B**ig **O**n **S**ecuring **S**uccess)

who has a _____ (**P**lease **L**earn **A**ll **N**ecessities) and makes _____

(**D**o **E**verything **M**anagement **A**sks, **N**o **D**iscussions) hopefully with an _____

(**I**nspiration **D**eserves **E**veryone's **A**ttention) that becomes a part of everyone's _____

(**D**esire **R**eflects **E**ventual **A**chievements **M**agically **S**ecured) increasing _____

(**C**hanging **O**ur **N**egative **F**ears **I**nvites **D**elightful **E**xperiences **N**ever **C**onsidered **E**asy) in everyone

to help them reach their potential!

- ## CHALLENGE

Producing results while abiding by the "Golden Rule"

1. Managing others while inspiring them to achieve:

➤ We are all managers, whether we are a child managing a game with other children or an adult leading a group of people in our area of expertise. An effective manager displays the ability to inspire others to achieve excellence. (check one in each group)

An effective manager should always:
___a. Intimidate the team to force the members into submission.
___b. Be a role model of displaying how character hopefully means; "Care how we act."
___c. Be very vindictive if questioned or corrected.
___d. All of the above.
___e. None of the above.

2. How to discover and procure respected role models:

➤ People view others in a multitude of different roles. All of us have the potential of being role models for a multitude of different reasons for many different people.

We discover our role models by:
___a. determining what we desire to accomplish.
___b. determining the level of involvement we wish to pursue.
___c. observing the level of success displayed by our role model.
___d. all of the above.
___e. all of the above.

We solidify our acceptance of our role models by:

    __a. the parallels we possess with our role model.
    __b. the respect others display toward our role model.
    __c. the amount of positive influence our role model radiates.
    __d. all of the above.
    __e. all of the above.

3. Turning a conflict into an inspirational opportunity:

➢ A very important skill for leaders to possess is the artistry to help people respectfully resolve conflicts. How do you respond when people experience conflicts with others and ask you to remedy the situation?

    __a. Help them rationalize that it is the other person's fault and to forget about it.
    __b. Tell the person that if they can't get it done, you'll find someone who can.
    __c. Tell the person the problem is their fault and not to bother you.
    __d. None of the above.
    __e. None of the above.

4. Inspiring others to voluntarily follow:

➢ The quintessential measure of successful leadership is convincing others to follow under their own volition. You would most likely follow a person voluntarily if that individual:

    __a. convinced you of the value and benefits you would receive because of your actions.
    __b. convinced you of the value and benefits others would receive because of your actions.
    __c. convinced you of the value and advantages you and others would receive because of your actions.
    __d. all of the above.
    __e. all of the above.

5. Helping others achieve success is integrity in action:

➢ The leader of an organization should:

    __a. gladly accept all of the accolades for the group's success.
    __b. exaggerate the problems the group created on their journey to success.
    __c. empower others to be successful, step back, and enjoy their celebration.
    __d. all of the above.
    __e. none of the above.

• CHANNEL

Integrity is ethical leadership in action

1. Managing others while inspiring them to achieve in an ethical manner:

➤ We are all leaders and followers depending on the situation. The CEO of a Fortune 500 company is certainly considered a boss and, hopefully, a leader at work. However, that person will be a humble follower when a preteen is teaching a lesson in the intricacies of the latest video game. Let's take a closer look at your opinions regarding ethical leadership.

Compare and select one of the two statements in each line to best complete the sentence below. Each line contains a positive and negative statement. Indicate your preference by placing a plus (+) by the statement you agree with, and place a minus (−) next to the statement you are not in agreement with.

"I would like a leader of mine to _____."

___act as a micromanager	___allow me to blossom
___offer me support	___intimidate me so I try harder
___earn my trust	___do anything it takes to succeed
___place the group's production first	___display ethical character
___inspire me to follow	___coerce me to produce
___rely on others to develop their skills	___help me develop my skills
___accept responsibility for decisions	___find someone to blame for problems
___insist on only absolute perfection	___help me correct my mistakes
___threaten me with punishment	___encourage me to improve
___decide everything for me	___when appropriate, ask my opinion
___complain often about other people	___praise people's accomplishments
___provide clear, concise directions	___get mad when I request clarification
___yell instructions at me	___simply tell me how to do it right
___often act very indecisively	___possibly help plan and prioritize my efforts
___make impractical demands to display power	___ask if I need help
___accept my excuses	___enforce expectations for production
___make me proud to associate with them	___be a model of how not to act
___make decisions based on moods	___always display balanced enthusiasm
___trust my judgment	___check on every detail of my efforts
___collaborate on action plans to reach goals	___use smoke and mirrors to mask facts
___become very vindictive if corrected	___apologize for mistakes
___be very approachable with problems	___blame the messenger for the problem
___spend energies fixing blame	___spend energies finding solutions
___very sincerely congratulate others	___take credit for other's achievements

___be remorseful, apologetic, and confused ___admit mistakes and plan for success

___attempt to wield power at every opportunity ___empower others as much as possible

___perpetually communicate a vision for success ___profess that bad stuff always just happens

___brag about accomplishments ___be a model of humility

___always work too hard ___inspire me to work expeditiously

___possess controlled intensity ___always seem to be upset

___not care about my lack of effort ___insist that I work hard to experience pride

___a very skilled communicator ___make me always wonder what's next

___ensure everyday is filled with surprises ___carry out plans very expeditiously

___let me know exactly what's expected ___depend on the moon phase and luck

___expect me to know everything ___help me learn and understand things

___be very competitive and pursue excellence ___value production over people

___insist that I reach my potential ___allow me to wallow in mediocrity

___listen to ideas with interest ___possess methods that are set in stone

___allow me to waste my breath in discussions ___care about me as a person

2. Developing into a respected leader and role model:

➤ Imagine you are leading a team of people in their quest to run a marathon, all 26.2 miles. Let's analyze the steps you would probably take in accomplishing this amazing feat for everyone's feet. What if we imagine your team has zero experience in running long distances? Which of the following steps might you take to help everyone complete a marathon in less than five hours?

Place a check on the appropriate answers:

___a. The team shows up at a marathon race, without any training, hoping to run the entire race.
___b. Everyone runs for 26.2 miles the day before the organized race in preparation for the event.
___c. Everybody loads up on carbohydrates for six months while preserving energy by not running.
___d. None of the above.

___a. Research running information and talk to experienced runners and coaches.
___b. Procure equipment from knowledgeable associates at reputable athletic stores.
___c. Point out the positive health benefits the team will receive by reaching their running potential.
___d. All of the above.

___a. On the first day of training simply walk a block then slowly run a block. Repeat four times.
___b. On the second day of training, walk two blocks, run two blocks. Repeat four times.
___c. On the third day of training, walk two blocks, run three blocks. Repeat four times.
___d. During the following training sessions simply add longer runs each day.
___e. All of the above.

___a. Run at a comfortable pace; the team members should be able to talk comfortably while running.
___b. Put a comfortable distance on everyone's legs every week; do one long run per week.
___c. Never run longer than twenty-five per cent more than the previous long run.
___d. All of the above.
___e. All of the above.

___a. Be properly hydrated.
___b. Be properly nourished.
___c. Be properly rested.
___d. All of the above.
___e. All of the above.

___a. Run in a safe environment at the most appropriate time of the day.
___b. Everyone should practice proper running form while maintaining a productive running schedule.
___c. Have fun training with other team members while celebrating everyone's progress.
___d. All of the above.
___e. All of the above.

3. Let's look at some of the big-picture topics you would explore to accomplish that feat:

➤ Check the appropriate topics that you would need to consider about running. You would probably investigate:

___a. who?
___b. why?
___c. what?
___d. when?
___e. where?
___f. how?
___g. all of the above.
___h. all of the above.

You would seek people out, possibly an organized running club, to discover (check the topics):

___a. where to run for training?
___b. how to be properly hydrated and nourished?
___c. the personal benefits your team will receive for accomplishing the feat.
___d. all of the above.
___e. all of the above.

You would make certain you understood the following topics (check the appropriate topics):

___a. shoes and clothing.
___b. running form and training schedule.
___c. the parallels between attaining success in running and your other activities.
___d. all of the above.
___e. all of the above.

4. Turning a conflict into an inspirational opportunity (check one):

➤ If someone complains to you about their lack of respect for a mutual acquaintances you should:

    ___a. tell them you'll work the problem out for them.
    ___b. argue with them and blame them for their accusations.
    ___c. tell them you are sure it's the other person's fault and not to worry about it.
    ___d. none of the above.
    ___e. none of the above.

    ___a. make certain you understand the lack of respect by asking questions to clarify the facts.
    ___b. repeat the facts back to them to make certain you have understood them correctly.
    ___c. avoid taking sides; tell them you understand that they are upset by the situation.
    ___d. all of the above.
    ___e. all of the above.

    ___a. ask them what steps they have taken to remedy the lack of respect thus far.
    ___b. if needed, help them develop an action plan to remedy the situation.
    ___c. set a future time for them to meet with you and explain their progress in resolving the problem.
    ___d. all of the above.
    ___e. all of the above.

5. Inspiring others to voluntarily follow:

➤ A boss can be a leader and a leader can be a boss. A boss can make demands until the preferred results are hopefully obtained, or the boss can inspire others to desire to produce the required results. Would you like to "have to do things" or would you rather "want to do things?" Life is certainly a balancing act of these two concepts. As an example, there are certainly lots of things that I "have wanted to do" rather than sit at this desk for the past two years working on this project. However, many times we "have to do things" to enable us to realize the personal PRIDE (People Respect Individuals Delivering Excellence) we receive by maximizing our potential.

Compare and select one of the two statements in each line to complete the sentence below. Each line contains a positive and a negative statement. Indicate your preference by placing a plus (+) by the statement you agree with and place a minus (−) next to the statement you are not in agreement with.

➤ "When I am in a position to lead I try to _____."

___act as a micromanager   ___allow others to blossom

___offer my support   ___intimidate them so they try harder

___have others earn my trust   ___do anything it takes to succeed

___place the group's production first   ___display ethical character

___inspire others to follow me   ___coerce others to produce for me

___rely on others to develop their skills   ___help people develop their skills

___accept responsibility for decisions   ___find someone to blame for problems

___insist on absolute perfection   ___accept and admit my mistakes

___threaten people with punishment   ___encourage others to improve ___decide everything for the group

___complain about other people

___provide clear, concise directions

___yell instructions at people

___often act very indecisively

___make impractical demands to display power

___accept excuses from people

___make them proud to associate with me

___make decisions based on moods

___trust other people's judgment

___collaborate on action plans to reach goals

___become very vindictive if corrected

___be very approachable with problems

___spend my energies fixing blame

___very sincerely congratulate others

___be remorseful, apologetic, and confused

___attempt to wield power at every opportunity

___perpetually communicate a vision for success

___accept excuses for low productivity

___possess controlled intensity

___be a very skilled communicator

___ensure every day is filled with surprises

___let others know exactly what's expected

___expect others to know everything

___insist others reach their potential

___be very competitive and model excellence

___accept excuses from others

___listen to ideas with interest

___care about others as individuals

___seek opinions, then decide

___praise people's accomplishments

___get mad if anyone requests clarification

___simply tell them how to do it right

___help plan and prioritize our efforts

___ask if I can help others understand

___carefully clarify their challenges

___be a control freak

___display balanced emotions

___check on every detail of their efforts

___use smoke and mirrors to mask facts

___apologize for my mistakes

___blame the messenger for the problem

___spend my energies finding solutions

___take credit for everyone's achievements

___admit mistakes and plan for success

___empower others as much as possible

___profess that bad stuff always just happens

___inspire others while demanding production

___always seem to be upset

___keep them asking lots of questions

___carry out plans very expeditiously

___depend on the moon phase for success

___help them learn and understand

___allow them to wallow in mediocrity

___value production over people

___enforce expectations for production

___prove my methods are set in stone

___allow others to waste their effort and time

(Add several more)

_____   _____

_____   _____

_____   _____

_____   _____

6. Helping others achieve success is integrity in action:

➤ List several people you know and the contributions they have made to lead others to success while displaying an extraordinary level of integrity. You might consider school experiences, sports teams, jobs, business organizations, community organizations, etc.

PEOPLE	ORGANIZATIONS	SUCCESSES

• CHECK

"Be like a postage stamp. Stick to one thing until you get there." —Josh Billings

• CONFIDENCE

Radiating kindness resonates

➤ List one or two goals on the following forms you wish to pursue to enhance your leadership skills.

ASSESSING GOALS*

*List your goal(s) and assign a number from 0 to 10 (10 being high)
to each consideration of the goals setting process.*

GOALS ➤➤➤➤➤➤➤➤➤ _____   _____

	(Primary Goal)	(Secondary Goal)
1. Level of need/passion	_____	_____
2. Level of desire to sacrifice	_____	_____
3. Level of research/planning	_____	_____
4. Level of action/skills	_____	_____
5. Ability to accept change	_____	_____
6. Ability to endure criticism	_____	_____
7. Available resources/assistance	_____	_____
8. Available time/energy	_____	_____
9. History of patience	_____	_____
10. History of commitment	_____	_____

Probability Index Total   _____   _____

Probability Index Scoring

90–100 . . . . . . Celebrate!   40–49 . . . . . . Should you reassess your goal?

80–89 . . . . Go for it!   30–39 . . . . . . Was your addition correct?

70–79 . . . . Have you analyzed obstacles?   20–29 . . . . . . Did you follow the directions?

60–69 . . . . Can you change anything?   10–19 . . . . . . Is it time for a reality check?

50–59 . . . . Is it worth the risk?   0–9 . . . . . . Possibly seek professional help?

*Greatness Only Awaits Labor…Staaaaaaaaaart!

_____
(CHAPTER TITLE)

_____
(GOAL/VISION/DREAM)

There is a need because:

_____
_____

The change, sacrifices and criticism that need to be addressed are:

_____
_____
_____

The assistance and resources that need to be procured are:

_____
_____

The history of patience and commitment has been:

_____
_____

In order to reach the goal I will:

_____
_____
_____
_____
_____
_____
_____

The beginning timeline is:

Set Goals	Planning	Implement	Completion?	Completed!
___/___/____	___/___/____	___/___/____	___/___/____	___/___/____

The celebration plans are:

_____
_____

_____

(CHAPTER TITLE)

_____

(GOAL/VISION/DREAM)

There is a need because:

_____

_____

The change, sacrifices and criticism that need to be addressed are:

_____

_____

_____

The assistance and resources that need to be procured are:

_____

_____

The history of patience and commitment has been:

_____

_____

In order to reach the goal I will:

_____

_____

_____

_____

_____

_____

The beginning timeline is:

Set Goals	Planning	Implement	Completion?	Completed!
___/___/___	___/___/___	___/___/___	___/___/___	___/___/___

The celebration plans are:

_____

_____

Indicate the acronyms that will help you achieve your goals.

BOSS	Big On Securing Success
BUSY	Bosses Usually Stress You
CONFIDENCE	Changing Our Negative Fears Invites Delightful Experiences Never Considered Easy
DEMAND	Do Everything Management Asks, No Discussion
DREAMS	Desire Reflects Eventual Achievements Magically Secured
EMPOWER	Everyone Makes Pertinent Observations With Every Response
ENJOY	Everyone Now Journey Over Yonder
FAIRLY	Fervent Attitudes Including Respect Lead You
IDEA	Inspiration Deserves Everyone's Attention
JOYS	Just Open Your Soul
JOYS	Just Offer Your Spirit
MUSIC	Mankind's Ultimate Study In Creation
NO	Nice Opportunity
PLAN	Please Learn All Necessities

INTEGRITY

www.CharacterConstructionCompany.com

ACROSS

3 Everybody Now Journey Over Yonder
4 Please Learn All Necessities
6 Inspiration Deserves Everyone's Attention
7 Everyone Makes Pertinent Observations With Every Response
9 Mankind's Ultimate Study In Creation
10 Just Open Your Soul
11 Nice Opportunity
12 Big On Securing Success

DOWN

1 Do Everything Management Asks; No Discussion
2 Changing Our Negative Fears Invites Delightful Experiences Never Considered Easy
5 Fervent Attitudes Including Respect Lead You
8 Bosses Usually Stress You
10 Just Offer Your Spirit

INTEGRITY

Find the words in the grid. When you are done, the unused letters in the grid will spell out a hidden message. Pick them out from left to right, top line to bottom line. Words can go horizontally, vertically and diagonally in all eight directions.

```
C  O  N  F  I  D  E  N  C  E
P  L  A  N  A  B  Y  E  I  D
S  Y  O  J  I  N  L  M  G  M
E  S  B  Y  T  I  R  P  H  U
N  S  D  E  D  Y  I  O  G  S
J  O  O  E  S  L  A  W  D  I
O  B  A  U  M  Y  F  E  E  C
Y  N  B  R  U  A  O  R  L  E
T  O  M  L  R  R  N  J  W  C
N  N  W  Y  N  C  J  D  R  M
```

www.CharacterConstructionCompany.com

BOSS	IDEA
BUSY	JOYS
CONFIDENCE	JOYS
DEMAND	MUSIC
EMPOWER	NO
ENJOY	PLAN
FAIRLY	

COMMUNICATION
Creating Only Manageable Methods,
Understanding Negative Innuendos Carefully,
And Teaming Individuals On Needs

• CONNECT
Discovering effective methods of sharing and understanding information

We instinctively like people who _____ (**S**ure **M**akes **I**t **L**ots **E**asier)

and are _____ (**N**ever **I**nsult **C**ompliment **E**veryone) to us.

We feel _____ (**N**otice **E**veryone's **E**steem **D**evelop **E**ach **D**ay)

when we share _____ (**H**elp **U**ndo **M**y **O**rdinary **R**esponse)

and avoid placing _____ (**B**ig **L**osers **A**lways **M**ake **E**xcuses)

by spreading _____ (**R**idicule **U**ndermines the **M**eaning **O**f **R**elationships)

and _____ (**G**uarded **O**ld **S**ecrets **S**ensationalized **I**n **P**ublic).

• CHALLENGE
Deciding when, where, and how to share what information with whom

1. Understanding the value of "wet working":

➤ Write the name of a person you would enjoy visiting to discuss a challenging project or activity.

_____   _____
(person's name or initials)   (project or activity)

➤ The person you listed has connections with about 200 people to potentially share your information. They have the possibility of generating nearly twice as much interest with their contacts than if you contact unfamiliar people. If the original 200 recipients of your information share it with 200 of their acquaintances, the number of people you can influence can exponentially reach 40,000 individuals. Is it becoming clearer why 70 percent of all jobs are discovered because of knowing others? Is it now apparent how anyone you would like to meet is only four or five people removed from you? Would you agree that we can maximize our leadership potential by properly designing, maintaining and refining our communication systems?

Research has revealed that communicating with only written words has 7 percent of the impact of meeting people face to face. Voice inflections add 38 percent effectiveness, and the impact of corresponding visual clues contributes 55 percent. Do these facts reflect the importance of sharing information via as many methods of effective communication as possible?

197

2. Analyzing why you appreciate being influenced by positive people who communicate effectively.

➤ Do you always thoroughly understand messages you receive from others?

____Yes

____No

➤ Can you absolutely guarantee that what you say and write is interpreted correctly?

____Yes

____No

➤ Would you like to learn more effective methods of imparting information to others?

____Yes

____No

3. Considering why you avoid negative people and situations:

➤ Take a few moments and estimate the number of people you attempt to avoid communicating with because of the negative impact of their messages. Write that estimated number of people on the line below.

_____
(number)

4. Adding more humor to your interactions with others:

William James said, "Common sense and a sense of humor is the same thing, moving at different speeds. A sense of humor is just common sense dancing."

➤ Humor is effective if it (check one):

____a. lightens up tense times and monotonous tasks.
____b. helps people get along with themselves and others better.
____c. doesn't interfere with respect and productivity.
____d. all of the above.
____e. all of the above.

➤ Humor is effective if it (check one):

____a. helps alleviate stress.
____b. shines a light of hope on difficult situations.
____c. improves health and mental stability.
____d. all of the above.
____e. all of the above.

➢ Humor is effective if it (check one):

    ___a. creates the possibility of hurting someone's feelings.
    ___b. belittles someone's race, name, gender, appearance, size, etc.
    ___c. belittles someone's abilities, beliefs, opinions, etc.
    ___d. none of the above.
    ___e. none of the above.

➢ Humor is effective if it (check one):

    ___a. wastes time.
    ___b. helps people understand.
    ___c. displays disrespect.
    ___d. all of the above.
    ___e. none of the above.

5. Understanding the basic principles of communication:

Two thousand years ago the Roman playwright Publilius Syrus wrote, "We are interested in others when they are interested in us." You would probably agree that human nature hasn't changed very much on that topic.

➢ We tend to like communicating with people who (check one):

    ___a. criticize us.
    ___b. compliment us.
    ___c. tell lies about us.
    ___d. all of the above.
    ___e. none of the above.

➢ We tend to like communicating with people who (check one):

    ___a. offend us.
    ___b. spread rumors about us.
    ___c. display their interest in us.
    ___d. all of the above.
    ___e. none of the above.

➢ We usually attempt to avoid communicating people who (check one):

    ___a. make us laugh.
    ___b. make us smile.
    ___c. insult us.
    ___d. all of the above.
    ___e. none of the above.

➢ We usually attempt to avoid communicating with people who (check one):

    ___a. care about us.
    ___b. fail to be interested in us.
    ___c. lead us to success.
    ___d. all of the above.
    ___e. none of the above.

6. Communicating effectively:

➤ Do you always practice proper patterns of communicating with others? Do you know people who habitually say things in ways that are grammatically incorrect and irritating? Imagine you are having a conversation with just one person, and the nearest other human being is miles away.

Place a plus (+) by what you would like to hear and say more often and a minus (−) by what you would like to hear and say less often from the pairs in the following listing.

__Are you asking me that question	__Thanks for asking the question
__Are you talking to me	__I appreciate hearing about
__My friends and I are going	__Me and my friends are going
__Sarah, Ralph, and I are going	__Me, Sarah, and Ralph are going
__I ain't got none	__I do not have any
__Uh, why, don't, uh, you	__Why don't you
__Where are you at	__Where are you
__I don't got to go because	__I don't have to go because
__I don't have any idea why	__I don't have no idea why
__Ya know, because, ya know	__Because you know that
__I don't have any	__I ain't got no
__I would like to know	__Like ya know, like things like just

(Add several more)

_____   _____

_____   _____

_____   _____

_____   _____

➤ Research has indicated the efficiency of only printed words to get a message across is (check one):

__a. about 7 percent.
__b. about 54 percent.
__c. about 77 percent.
__d. all of the above.
__e. none of the above.

➤ Research has indicated the efficiency of using tone of voice, voice inflection, and other sounds to impart a message is (check one):

__a. about 38 percent.
__b. about 18 percent.
__c. about 7 percent.
__d. all of the above.
__e. none of the above.

➤ Research has discovered that the efficiency of using nonverbal communication to get a message across face to face is (check one):

    ___a. about 55 percent.
    ___b. about 27 percent.
    ___c. about 7 percent.
    ___d. all of the above.
    ___e. none of the above.

➤ Research indicates the single most effective method of delivering a message in person is (check one):

    ___a. nonverbal.
    ___b. sounds.
    ___c. words.
    ___d. all of the above.
    ___e. none of the above.

➤ Research has shown the most effective method of imparting a message is (check one):

    ___a. all of the answers to the letter a. above (clue-do the math).
    ___b. all of the answers to the letter b. above.
    ___c. all of the answers to the letter c. above.
    ___d. all of the above.
    ___e. none of the above.

7. Learning to endure criticism (check one):

➤ Enduring criticism can be accomplished by:

    ___a. avoiding an instant confrontation with the source of the criticism.
    ___b. attempting to understand the reasoning behind the criticism.
    ___c. breathing through your nose for at least ten seconds to avoid arguing.
    ___d. all of the above.
    ___e. all of the above.

8. Avoiding the urge to provide too much information (check one):

➤ When you are tempted to divulge WTMI (**W**ay **T**oo **M**uch **I**nformation) you should always remember:

    ___a. you can resist anything except temptation.
    ___b. think of the absolute worst outcome of your actions.
    ___c. how the information can be embellished and passed on.
    ___d. all of the above.
    ___e. all of the above.

9. Being aware of imparting inappropriate information (check one):

➤ When deciding to impart inappropriate information about someone you should always:
    ___a. not do it.
    ___b. not do it.
    ___c. not do it.
    ___d. all of the above.
    ___e. all of the above.

10. Quelling rumors and gossip (check one):

➤ To minimize untrue stories it is best to:

    ___a. be extremely careful of what you say to whom.
    ___b. be aware of who is overhearing or has access to the information.
    ___c. not repeat something you shouldn't, so just breathe through your nose.
    ___d. all of the above.
    ___e. all of the above.

11. Enduring failed communications (check one):

➤ Review the situation and attempt to determine:

    ___a. what information was shared.
    ___b. who received the information.
    ___c. what would be more efficient in the future.
    ___d. all of the above.
    ___e. all of the above.

• CHANNEL

Understanding how we are most effective in sharing information with others

1. You probably agree that we receive information via words, voice inflections, and visual clues. Let's analyze how we might best use these forms of communication to successfully convey information.

➤ Imagine one of your acquaintances will contact you electronically in the next few minutes and ask, "What's happening, friend?"

➤ You would probably tell them:

    ___a. where you are.
    ___b. what you are doing.
    ___c. why you are doing what you are doing.
    ___d. all of the above.
    ___e. all of the above.

➤ You would probably also tell them:

    ___a. who you are with.
    ___b. how you're doing.
    ___c. when you'll be done.
    ___d. all of the above.
    ___e. all of the above.

➤ Using the above information of where, what, why, who, how, and when, write a short paragraph to your friend to tell them "what's happening."

_____

_____

_____

_____

_____

_____

_____

_____

_____

_____

2. Analyzing why we appreciate being influenced by positive people and why we avoid associating with negative people:

➤ Place a plus sign (+) next to the words you would like to end the following sentence with and place a minus (−) by the words that you would not like to hear end this sentence.

➤ "I appreciate and look forward to communicating with people when they help me

   feel _____"

__conspicuous	__argumentative	__intimidated	__motivated	__happy
__important	__valuable	__stupid	__skillful	__klutzy
__humorous	__unattractive	__curious	__at ease	__trustworthy
__useful	__ineffective	__smart	__attractive	__talented
__slow	__reclusive	__loved	__proud	__appreciated
__inefficient	__productive	__enjoyable	__confident	__deceitful
__precious	__unworthy	__happy	__sad	__self-conscious
__upset	__empowered	__drained	__stressed	__tired
__enthusiastic	__depressed	__intelligent	__needed	__worthless
__credible	__energized	__efficient	__motivated	__dumb
__humble	__sad	__fearful	__witty	__calm
__successful	__nervous	__relaxed	__secure	__stymied
__guilty	__worthy	__confused	__inferior	__anxious

___special	___angry	___invited	___welcome	___defensive
___withdrawn	___creative	___successful	___smart	___fulfilled
___able	___argumentative	___intimidated	___flexible	___fatigued

(Add several more)

_____ _____ _____ _____ _____

_____ _____ _____ _____ _____

_____ _____ _____ _____ _____

3. Considering why you try to avoid specific people and situations:

➤ Did acquaintances of yours come to mind while you were marking the previous list?

___Yes

___No

➤ Is it becoming clearer how we select people we wish to communicate with?

___Yes

___No

➤ Might one of the roadblocks to effective communications simply be that we avoid certain people because of the way they influence our self confidence?

___Yes

___No

4. Adding more humor to your interactions with others (check one):

➤ Some effective methods of adding humor to your interactions are:

 ___a. making an inoffensive pun.
 ___b. making an innocent play on words.
 ___c. adding to the inoffensive humor of others.
 ___d. all of the above.
 ___e. all of the above.

➤ Effective avenues for helping develop appropriate humor are:

 ___a. associating with humorous role models.
 ___b. reading appropriate humor in books, magazines, online, etc.
 ___c. trying to acknowledge the humorous aspects of everyday life.
 ___d. all of the above.
 ___e. all of the above.

5. Recognizing the benefits of effective communication (check one in each section):

➤ Conflicts commonly occur when:

    ___a. messages are misunderstood.
    ___b. messages are not fully explained.
    ___c. the message recipient avoids active listening and understanding.
    ___d. all of the above.
    ___e. all of the above.

➤ You will have more confidence for imparting your information to groups by:

    ___a. being convinced of the value of the message.
    ___b. concentrating on the importance of the message.
    ___c. imagining you are speaking to a close friend.
    ___d. all of the above.
    ___e. all of the above.

➤ You can gain confidence for speaking in front of groups by:

    ___a. practicing in front of a mirror.
    ___b. practicing to an imaginary audience in an empty room.
    ___c. practicing in the presentation room in advance.
    ___d. all of the above.
    ___e. all of the above.

➤ You can develop more confidence for speaking in front of groups by:

    ___a. practicing while imagining you are talking in front of a group.
    ___b. imagining the group is enjoying your presentation.
    ___c. imagining the group is giving you an ovation at the conclusion of the talk.
    ___d. all of the above.
    ___e. all of the above.

6. Communicating effectively via a variety of methods (check one in each section):

➤ When sending electronic mail while representing an organization you should:

    ___a. treat it as though you are sending personal mail from home.
    ___b. make it more tantalizing by adding numerous hidden messages and innuendos.
    ___c. abide by company policies, rules, and guidelines.
    ___d. all of the above.
    ___e. none of the above.

➤ You should try to avoid sending emails that involve:

    ___a. delegating others to accomplish less than desirable tasks.
    ___b. sensitive information that should remain confidential.
    ___c. email critical of the recipient.
    ___d. all of the above.
    ___e. all of the above.

➤ You should try to avoid sending negative emails because:

    ___a. unhappy people spread their feelings more freely than happy people.
    ___b. original emails can be tracked, saved, edited, embellished, and forwarded.
    ___c. it's nearly impossible to effectively relate messages with only words.
    ___d. all of the above.
    ___e. all of the above.

➤ Before you send an email you should always try to:

    ___a. edit the text from your perspective.
    ___b. edit the text from the perspective of the intended recipient(s).
    ___c. wait a while before you send it, especially if you are upset.
    ___d. all of the above.
    ___e. all of the above.

➤ When you receive a personal or business related email you should:

    ___a. avoid responding for at least one week.
    ___b. respond very soon with at least a "Thanks," or an "I'll try to find out," etc.
    ___c. respond that you don't appreciate being bothered.
    ___d. all of the above.
    ___e. none of the above.

➤ When you send an email to someone it is impossible to know:

    ___a. the mood of the recipient and their emotional reaction.
    ___b. the stresses being experienced by the recipient.
    ___c. if they are able to respond in a timely fashion.
    ___d. all of the above.
    ___e. all of the above.

➤ When you send an email keep in mind it is impossible to:

    ___a. guarantee the recipient's interpretation of the message.
    ___b. impart the appropriate tone and inflection of the words.
    ___c. always have a clear view of the recipient's reactions.
    ___d. all of the above.
    ___e. all of the above.

➤ When writing a message attempt to:

    ___a. add a sense of mystery; mention only some of the clues regarding the subject.
    ___b. write clearly by listing: who, what, where, when, why, and how.
    ___c. confuse the recipient so they will desire to search for the facts.
    ___d. all of the above.
    ___e. none of the above.

➢ If you receive an email message of a critical nature you should:

    ___a. respond immediately with proof that you are right and the sender is wrong.
    ___b. forward altered copies to as many people as possible.
    ___c. call the person on the phone; better yet, meet face-to-face.
    ___d. all of the above.
    ___e. none of the above.

➢ The most effective method of imparting information and receiving feedback is to:

    ___a. provide a plethora of emails to everyone you know on a consistent basis.
    ___b. entertain everyone with the latest and greatest jokes and cute stories.
    ___c. use email sparingly; try to meet face-to-face to effectively share information.
    ___d. all of the above.
    ___e. none of the above.

➢ Proper cell phone usage is an evolving communications issue and an essential social skill. Place a plus (+) next to what is acceptable in each line to end the sentence below and a minus (−) next to improper cell phone etiquette.

➢ "Cell phones ideally should be used _____."

___while having a face-to-face discussion   ___if you are not talking to someone in person

___while you are near other people   ___if you are in a quiet place away from others

___while you are in an audience   ___after an event has concluded or at a break

___by speaking loud and clear   ___in normal conversational tones

___with loud ring tones to impress others   ___with the sound off while in group settings

___by regularly checking your messages   ___by ignoring messages while with others

___during a presentation   ___before, after, or during a break from the event

___by wearing your earpiece fulltime   ___by using the earpiece while away from others

___while using machinery   ___while on a break from work

___while steering a car, bike, scooter, etc.   ___while in a safe environment

___when your organization's policy allows   ___whenever you wish

_____   _____

_____   _____

➢ The Olympic gymnast Mary Lou Retton has said, "You know right away if someone is approachable or not. You can read a person by nonverbal communication and body language . . . and you know when they don't want to be talked to."

➢ Understanding that using only words is a very difficult and ineffective method of getting messages across is a major step toward effective communication. Are you beginning to understand why we spend so much time learning how to select the precise words to convey our ideas?

A perfect example of understanding the impact of nonverbal communication is analyzing the advent of the movie industry. A century ago movie buffs filled theaters to simply "watch" people act on screen as a pianist or an orchestra performed. In the 1920s when sound and dialogue were added to the movies, a strange phenomenon occurred. Many of the most famous actors and actresses became ineffective with using words and fell from their starring roles.

➤ Place a check mark on your guess of the usual meaning of the following actions:

Folded arms usually indicates:
___happiness
___being defensive

Open palms usually indicates:
___anger
___honesty

Rubbing eyes usually indicates:
___considering options
___being deceitful

Picking at lint on clothing usually indicates:
___preparing to tell the truth
___disapproval of what is being said

Hands behind head usually indicates:
___nervousness, being submissive
___dominance, in control

Mirroring gestures usually indicates:
___defiance
___agreement

Smiling usually indicates:
___a recent trip to the dentist
___acceptance

Glancing down usually indicates:
___confidence
___lying

Tight jaw usually indicates:
___hungry
___upset

Purposely seated on opposite sides of table or desk usually indicates:
___cooperation
___being defensive

7. Learning to endure criticism (check one):

➢ To avoid unfairly criticizing others you can:

    ___a. ask them if they know what they did wrong.
    ___b. ask them if they have an idea that will be more effective.
    ___c. ask them if they'd like you to help them discover the correct answer.
    ___d. all of the above.
    ___e. all of the above.

➢ To fairly criticize others you can:

    ___a. tell them they are stupid.
    ___b. blame it on their gender.
    ___c. blame it on their race.
    ___d. none of the above.
    ___e. none of the above.

8. Avoiding the urge to provide too much information (check one):

➢ Confidentiality is an extremely important attribute of human interaction. To ensure that information you relate to others is necessary you should always ask yourself:

    ___a. if the person was listening, would I divulge this information?
    ___b. if the person's attorney was here, would I divulge this information?
    ___c. if a television news crew was filming this, would I continue?
    ___d. all of the above.
    ___e. all of the above.

9. Being aware of imparting inappropriate information (check one):

➢ Before you say anything about anybody always ask yourself:

    ___a. is it true?
    ___b. is it kind?
    ___c. is it necessary?
    ___d. all of the above.
    ___e. all of the above.

10. Quelling rumors and gossip:

➢ Place a plus (+) next to the actions you should take and a minus (−) next to the actions you should avoid.

If there is an untrue rumor or unfair gossip being spread I should:

___Attempt to determine if it is true.

___Attempt to determine the origin of the story.

___Threaten the perpetrator with the potential of starting a rumor about them.

___Attempt to determine the intent of the perpetrator.

___Argue with the originator of the story.

___Ask the originator if they need clarification of the situation.

___Seek advice for "damage control."

___Determine what resolution I would like to attain.

___Seek help in resolving the fallacious drama.

___Offer to provide the originator with money if they retract the rumor.

___Determine how long I am willing to pursue quelling the information.

___Depending on the severity of the information, possibly seek legal assistance.

11. Checking your communication skills you exercise with others:

➤ Answer the following statements "yes" with a plus (+) or "no" with a minus (−).

➤ "Others know that I will:

___greet them with an open mind."

___attempt to be available for them."

___respond in a timely manner."

___compliment them for displaying a concern."

___hear all of their concerns without interrupting."

___ask questions when they are done to make certain I understand their perspective."

___repeat their message to determine if I understand it correctly."

___ask if they have suggestions for resolving the situation."

___tell them not to bother me."

___respect their opinion, even if I disagree."

___protect their innermost secrets."

___explode in anger when they tell me their problems."

___listen to only some of their suggestions."

___tell them I appreciate their suggestions."

___let them know if it is beyond my power to follow their suggestion."

___suggest who they might turn to for further help."

___attempt to understand their opinions."

___unduly criticize their opinions."

___unduly criticize their opinions to others."

___avoid being the spokesperson for the parties involved."

___be receptive regarding information from 'anonymous sources.'"

___help them develop options to provide a resolution."

___explain my concept of options without arguing."

___explain my opinions without arguing."

___try to offer suggestions rather than fix blame."

___attempt to arrive at an agreeable solution."

___analyze possible outcomes for future planning."

___potentially 'role play' to help everyone understand."

___approach their desires from their viewpoint."

___attempt to help everyone maintain a spirit of cooperation."

___work on developing trusting relationships."

___be a respectful negotiator analyzing facts, more than personalities."

___bring clarity to conflicts, strengthening relationships in the process."

___consider individual differences and strengths while forming opinions."

___treat everyone fairly, regardless of how I feel about them personally."

___put myself in their situation and try to determine the outcome I would appreciate."

___respect everyone's personal dignity."

___offer facts not attacks, help not harass, care not crush."

___maintain open avenues for future communications."

_____ "

_____ "

_____ "

_____ "

- **CHECK**

  "The greatest problem in communication is the illusion that it has been accomplished." —George Bernard Shaw

- **CONFIDENCE**

  Communication is a boomerang; what comes back is what really counts!

  ➢ List one or two goals on the following forms that will help you become more successful in communicating with others.

ASSESSING GOALS*

*List your goal(s) and assign a number from 0 to 10 (10 being high)
to each consideration of the goals setting process.*

GOALS ➤➤➤➤➤➤➤➤➤ _____ _____
                              (Primary Goal)   (Secondary Goal)

1. Level of need/passion	____	____
2. Level of desire to sacrifice	____	____
3. Level of research/planning	____	____
4. Level of action/skills	____	____
5. Ability to accept change	____	____
6. Ability to endure criticism	____	____
7. Available resources/assistance	____	____
8. Available time/energy	____	____
9. History of patience	____	____
10. History of commitment	____	____

Probability Index Total   ____   ____

Probability Index Scoring

90–100 . . . . . . Celebrate!   40–49 . . . . . . Should you reassess your goal?
80–89 . . . . Go for it!   30–39 . . . . . . Was your addition correct?
70–79 . . . . Have you analyzed obstacles?   20–29 . . . . . . Did you follow the directions?
60–69 . . . . Can you change anything?   10–19 . . . . . . Is it time for a reality check?
50–59 . . . . Is it worth the risk?   0–9 . . . . . . Possibly seek professional help?

*Greatness Only Awaits Labor…Staaaaaaaaaart!

(GOAL/VISION/DREAM)

There is a need because:

_____

_____

The change, sacrifices and criticism that need to be addressed are:

_____

_____

_____

The assistance and resources that need to be procured are:

_____

_____

The history of patience and commitment has been:

_____

_____

In order to reach the goal I will:

_____

_____

_____

_____

_____

_____

_____

The beginning timeline is:

Set Goals	Planning	Implement	Completion?	Completed!
___/___/____	___/___/____	___/___/____	___/___/____	___/___/____

The celebration plans are:

_____

_____

_____

(CHAPTER TITLE)

_____

(GOAL/VISION/DREAM)

There is a need because:

_____

_____

The change, sacrifices and criticism that need to be addressed are:

_____

_____

_____

The assistance and resources that need to be procured are:

_____

_____

The history of patience and commitment has been:

_____

_____

In order to reach the goal I will:

_____

_____

_____

_____

_____

_____

_____

The beginning timeline is:

Set Goals	Planning	Implement	Completion?	Completed!
___/___/_____	___/___/_____	___/___/_____	___/___/_____	___/___/_____

The celebration plans are:

_____

_____

Indicate the acronyms that will help you achieve your goals.

ANGER	Acclaiming Negative Garbage Eradicates Relationships
BLAME	Big Losers Always Make Excuses
BS	Back Stabbing, Bad Stuff, Be Sincere
GOSSIP	Guarded Old Secrets Sensationalized In Public
HUMOR	Help Undo My Ordinary Response
LAUGH	Levity Always Underscores Good Habits
LUCK	Languishing Using Current Knowledge
MAD	Meanness Always Destroys
NEEDED	Notice Everyone's Esteem Develop Each Day
NICE	Never Insult, Compliment Everyone
OOPS	Opportunities Often Pass Swiftly
PRACTICE	Perfecting Repeated Actions Considerably, To Increase Confidence Every time
RUMOR	Ridicule Undermines the Meaning Of Relationships
SMILE	Sure Makes It Lots Easier
SPAM	Some People Are Mean
WTMI	Way Too Much Information

COMMUNICATION

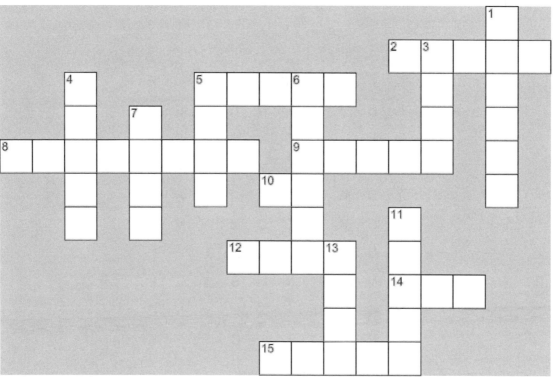

www.CharacterConstructionCompany.com.com

ACROSS

2 Acclaiming Negative Garbage Eradicates Relationships

5 Levity Always Underscores Good Habits

8 Perfecting Repeated Actions Considerably, To Increase Confidence Everytime

9 Sure Makes It Lots Easier

10 Back Stabbing Bad Stuff Be Sincere

12 Opportunities Often Pass Swiftly

14 Meanness Always Destroys

15 Help Undo My Ordinary Response

DOWN

1 Notice Everyone's Esteem Develop Each Day

3 Never Insult Compliment Everyone

4 Big Losers Always Make Excuses

5 Languishing Using Current Knowledge

6 Guarded Old Secrets Sensationalized In Public

7 Way Too Much Information

11 Ridicule Undermines Meaning Of Relationships

13 Some People Are Mean

COMMUNICATION

Find the words in the grid. When you are done, the unused letters in the grid will spell out a hidden message. Pick them out from left to right, top line to bottom line. Words can go horizontally, vertically and diagonally in all eight directions.

```
O  O  P  S  R  R  U  M  O  R
K  C  U  L  E  N  E  V  E  D
D  R  I  C  G  N  E  B  S  E
S  A  I  U  N  M  L  L  P  D
T  N  M  G  A  S  A  C  A  E
O  H  M  L  O  U  M  W  M  E
P  U  B  L  G  S  T  I  I  N
M  M  E  H  N  M  S  T  L  E
V  O  E  R  I  Y  O  I  N  E
P  R  A  C  T  I  C  E  P  E
```

ANGER	NEEDED
BLAME	NICE
BS	OOPS
GOSSIP	PRACTICE
HUMOR	RUMOR
LAUGH	SMILE
LUCK	SPAM
MAD	WTMI

SUCCESS

Seek Understanding Carefully;
Character Eventually Sows Satisfaction

- ## CONNECT

  Defining a successful life

  Success in _____ (**L**ove **I**s **F**or **E**veryone) might be as simple as learning to have

  _____ (**F**orget **U**nnecessary **N**onsense) while we _____ (**T**o **R**espect **Y**ourself)

  to achieve _____ (**P**racticing **E**ffective **A**ttitudes **C**alms **E**veryone) of mind by

  leaving a _____ (**L**et **E**very **G**ift **A**ttribute **C**ompliments to **Y**ou) of sharing our

  _____ (**W**ishing **E**veryone **A**chieves **L**ove'n **T**otal **H**appiness) with others.

- ## CHALLENGE

  Understanding the struggles and joys of success

  1. Learning to perpetually keep trying:

  ➢ When you try and don't like the outcome, just try again.

     Relate a situation in your life where you overcame failure because you simply kept trying.

  _____

  _____

  _____

  _____

  _____

  _____

  _____

  _____

  _____

2. Overlooking past failures:

➤ Accepting failure can be viewed as learning what to avoid in the future.

> Explain what failures you have let go of in your life to allow yourself to successfully proceed.

_____

_____

_____

_____

_____

_____

3. Studying role models' paths to success:

➤ Carefully study what others have done to be successful.

> What traits has your role model inspired you to use the most?

_____

_____

_____

_____

_____

4. Developing patience, commitment, faith, and tolerance:

➤ Acquiring personal traits required for success.

> What have you tolerated the most to allow yourself to be successful?

_____

_____

_____

_____

_____

5. Learning to work hard:

➢ Developing a work ethic based on sacrifice and perpetually trying.

What has been your most significant sacrifice to allow yourself to be successful?

_____

_____

_____

_____

_____

6. Understanding the implications of the word wealth:

➢ Wealth means much more than accumulating cash.

List the "treasures" that you possess in your life.

_____

_____

_____

_____

_____

_____

• CHANNEL

Learning to apply concepts leading to success

1. Learning to perpetually keep trying:

➢ Describe a long sought after goal that you successfully attained.

_____

_____

_____

_____

2. Overlooking past failures:

➤ Explain a goal you continue to pursue and hope to attain in the future.

_____

_____

_____

_____

_____

3. Studying role models' paths to success:

➤ Let's analyze what Tiger Woods, Peyton Manning, Serena Williams, Warren Buffet, and Thomas Edison have in common.

   Do you think Tiger Woods has missed more golf shots than you have?
   Do you think Peyton Manning has lost more football games than you have?
   Do you think Serena Williams has hit the net with a tennis ball more than you have?
   Do you think Warren Buffet has lost more investment money than you have?
   Do you think Thomas Edison had more unsuccessful inventions than you have?

➤ The five people mentioned have all failed at these things more than I have because they have all tried them (check one):

   ___a. about the same as I have.
   ___b. more than I have.
   ___c. less than I have.

➤ Because they have tried more than I have they have also (check one):

   ___a. been more unsuccessful at them than I have.
   ___b. been more successful at them than I have.
   ___c. been about as successful at them as I have.

3. Developing patience, commitment, faith, and tolerance:

   Commitment, faith, and tolerance are required to develop patience with yourself and others. The first challenge in developing patience is to decide if you can forgo your insecurities and believe that your goals are worth the effort and sacrifice. An immense help in developing patience is visualizing the outcome and benefits of the success at hand.

➤ Explain a situation you have experienced where you were able to practice patience to help lead others to success.

_____

_____

_____

_____

_____

5. Learning to work hard consists of displaying habits that lead to success:

➤ Match the following success traits with their opposites and then add several that you feel are important for you.

1) ____ Visionary		A) Selfish
2) ____ Enthusiastic		B) Inconsistent
3) ____ Organized		C) Tubular vision
4) ____ Reliable		D) Lackadaisical
5) ____ Confident		E) Procrastinator
6) ____ Positive		F) Quitter
7) ____ Compassionate		G) Inflexible
8) ____ Creative		H) Judgmental
9) ____ Honest		I) Fearful
10) ____ Resilient		J) Deceptive
11) __ _____		K) _____
12) __ _____		L) _____
13) __ _____		M) _____
14) __ _____		N) _____
15) __ _____		O) _____

7. Understanding the implications of the word wealth:

➤ Imagine you are the richest person in the world; list some of the things you would like to buy and the places you would like to travel to spend lots and lots and lots of your money.

PURCHASES	PLACES
_____	_____
_____	_____
_____	_____
_____	_____
_____	_____

➤ Imagine you could win anything that you tried to win and you could be famous for anything that you wanted to be famous for accomplishing; list them.

WINNINGS	FAMOUS FOR
_____	_____
_____	_____
_____	_____
_____	_____
_____	_____

➤ List the people you have personally known (still on earth or not) with whom you would like to share your money, winnings, fame, and travels.

PEOPLE	PEOPLE
_____	_____
_____	_____
_____	_____
_____	_____
_____	_____

➤ Here it comes: Let's see how your **GPS** (**G**o **P**laces **S**uccessfully) is functioning. Place the following words in numerical order to display how you prioritize their importance in your life.

        ____**C**ompetition

        ____**A**cclaim

        ____**M**oney

        ____**P**eople

➤ Your final examination: Complete the following acronym.

W_____

E_____

A_____

L_____

T_____

H_____

• CHECK

"If you work just for money, you'll never make it. But if you love what you are doing…success will be yours." —**Ray Kroc**

• CONFIDENCE

"Success is not counted by how high you have climbed but by how many you have brought with you." —**Bob Moawad**

➤ List two goals on the following forms that will hopefully bring more love and happiness to your life.

ASSESSING GOALS*

*List your goal(s) and assign a number from 0 to 10 (10 being high)
to each consideration of the goals setting process.*

GOALS ➤➤➤➤➤➤➤➤➤ _____   _____
(Primary Goal)   (Secondary Goal)

	Primary Goal	Secondary Goal
1. Level of need/passion	_____	_____
2. Level of desire to sacrifice	_____	_____
3. Level of research/planning	_____	_____
4. Level of action/skills	_____	_____
5. Ability to accept change	_____	_____
6. Ability to endure criticism	_____	_____
7. Available resources/assistance	_____	_____
8. Available time/energy	_____	_____
9. History of patience	_____	_____
10. History of commitment	_____	_____

Probability Index Total   _____   _____

Probability Index Scoring

90–100 . . . . . . Celebrate!
80–89 . . . . Go for it!
70–79 . . . . Have you analyzed obstacles?
60–69 . . . . Can you change anything?
50–59 . . . . Is it worth the risk?

40–49 . . . . . . Should you reassess your goal?
30–39 . . . . . . Was your addition correct?
20–29 . . . . . . Did you follow the directions?
10–19 . . . . . . Is it time for a reality check?
0–9 . . . . . . Possibly seek professional help?

*Greatness Only Awaits Labor…Staaaaaaaaaart!

_____

(CHAPTER TITLE)

_____

(GOAL/VISION/DREAM)

There is a need because:

_____

_____

The change, sacrifices and criticism that need to be addressed are:

_____

_____

_____

The assistance and resources that need to be procured are:

_____

_____

The history of patience and commitment has been:

_____

_____

In order to reach the goal I will:

_____

_____

_____

_____

_____

_____

_____

The beginning timeline is:

Set Goals	Planning	Implement	Completion?	Completed!
___/___/_____	___/___/_____	___/___/_____	___/___/_____	___/___/_____

The celebration plans are:

_____

_____

_____

(CHAPTER TITLE)

_____

(GOAL/VISION/DREAM)

There is a need because:

_____

_____

The change, sacrifices and criticism that need to be addressed are:

_____

_____

_____

The assistance and resources that need to be procured are:

_____

_____

The history of patience and commitment has been:

_____

_____

In order to reach the goal I will:

_____

_____

_____

_____

_____

_____

The beginning timeline is:

Set Goals	Planning	Implement	Completion?	Completed!
___/___/_____	___/___/_____	___/___/_____	___/___/_____	___/___/_____

The celebration plans are:

_____

_____

Indicate which acronyms will help you achieve success.

BORED	Bring On Remembrances Every Day
CONFIDENCE	Changing Our Negative Fears Invites Delightful Experiences Never Considered Easy
DREAMS	Desire Reflects Eventual Achievements Magically Secured
FUN	Forget Unnecessary Nonsense
HAPPY	Have All the Peace 'n Pleasure Ya want
HOME	Happiness Only Means Everything
LEGACY	Let Every Gift Attribute Compliments to You
LIFE	Love Is For Everyone
LOVE	Lights On, Very Empowering
LUCK	Languishing Using Current Knowledge
PEACE	Practicing Effective Attitudes Calms Everyone
TRUTH	To Rely Upon Their Honor
TRY	To Respect Yourself
WEALTH	Wishing Everyone Achieves Love 'n Total Happiness

SUCCESS

www.CharacterConstructionCompany.com

ACROSS

2 Love Is For Everyone

5 Happiness Only Means Everything

7 Changing Our Negative Fears Invites Delightful Experiences Never Considered Easy

9 To Respect Yourself

10 Desire Reflects Eventual Achievements Magically Secured

11 Forget Unnecessary Nonsense

12 Languishing Using Current Knowledge

13 Have All the Peace'n Pleasure Y'Want

DOWN

1 Practicing Effective Attitudes Calms Everyone

3 Lights On Very Empowering

4 Let Every Gift Attribute Compliments to You

6 Bring On Remembrances Every Day

8 Wishing Everyone Achieves Love'n Total Happiness

9 To Rely Upon Their Honor

SUCCESS

Find the words in the grid. When you are done, the unused letters in the grid will spell out a hidden message. Pick them out from left to right, top line to bottom line. Words can go horizontally, vertically and diagonally in all eight directions.

```
C  T  R  U  T  H  O  M  H  E
P  F  P  E  A  C  E  O  C  V
W  D  U  E  T  K  M  N  I  O
H  E  T  N  C  E  E  I  O  L
A  R  A  U  N  D  A  C  C  L
P  O  L  L  I  E  T  A  I  M
P  B  M  F  T  O  F  R  N  E
Y  Y  N  O  R  H  P  I  Y  E
O  O  D  R  E  A  M  S  L  P
C  L  E  R  Y  C  A  G  E  L
```

www.CharacterConstructionCompany.com

BORED	LIFE
CONFIDENCE	LOVE
DREAMS	LUCK
FUN	PEACE
HAPPY	TRUTH
HOME	TRY
LEGACY	WEALTH

About the Author

Bruce Brummond has helped thousands develop their SELF-WORTH (Securing Esteem Lessens Fear, Working Offers Respect Triggering Happiness) while maximizing their potential to achieve SUCCESS (Seek Understanding Carefully, Character Eventually Sows Satisfaction). He has shared his talents as a salesman, commercial fisherman, competitive bass fisherman, music educator, school district administrator, author, and "moti-vacational" speaker.

Bruce is the owner and founder of Character Construction Company, an organization dedicated to assisting individuals and organizations throughout the world enhance their INTEGRITY (Individuals Never Trust Evil, Golden Rule Inspires Their Years) while reaching their GOALS (Greatness Only Awaits Labor…Start!)

The Book . . .

    1.   *Acronyms Building Character, the ABC's of Life*

The Workbook . . .

    2.   *Character Building Acronyms, the ABC's at Work*

The Poster of Skipper that says . . .

    3.   *SOUL—Source Of Unconditional Love*

Can be ordered at. . .

www.Atlasbooks.com or by calling 1-800BOOKLOG

Contact Bruce Brummond at:

www.characterconstructioncompany.com
bruce@characterconstructioncompany.com